# The good (but cheap) Chicago Restaurant Book

# The good (but cheap) Chicago Restaurant Book

**Where to Find Great Meals at Little Neighborhood Restaurants From $1.50 to $4.50**

Jill & Ron Rohde

THE SWALLOW PRESS INC.
CHICAGO

Printed in the United States of America

Published by
The Swallow Press Incorporated
1139 South Wabash Avenue
Chicago, Illinois 60605

First Printing September 1974

This book is printed on recycled paper

LIBRARY OF CONGRESS CATALOG NUMBER 74–12945
ISBN 0–8040–0673–3

## Acknowledgments

For help on this book, there are almost too many mouths to thank. Foremost are John, Neal, Larry, Evie, and Don.

Special thanks to Donna, Nancy, Jim, Barbara, Phyllis, Lorrie, and Diane, and to countless others for their advice, tips, and encouragement.

Interior illustrations by Darby Holmes.

# Table of Contents

# Introduction

To us, Chicago is its many distinctive neighborhoods and, of course, the people in them. Where else could you find the same energy, diversity, and flavor of a Halsted Street, Milwaukee Avenue, or Cermak Road? One of the amazing things about the city is that the melting pot has never stopped bubbling. Just when it seemed as though almost everyone had either quietly assimilated or else forsaken the city for suburbia, in came new groups of Greeks, Thais, Indians, Koreans, Philippinos, Colombians, Puerto Ricans, and Arabs. Settling into their own neighborhoods, these new arrivals have added a slew of good ethnic restaurants to the list of Italian, German, French, Swedish, Bohemian, Chinese, Mexican, and Japanese.

We've found that one of the best and easily the most pleasant ways to capture the feel and beauty of a neighborhood is to eat in it. While we've always been interested in discovering little, out-of-the-way restaurants, this past year has been one of exploring Chicago from one end to the other, seeking out places where the people go for authentic home cooking at friendly prices. We've eaten potato kugel in Albany Park, lasagna on Taylor Street, moussaka on Lawrence Avenue, cranberry-filled pancakes in Marquette Park, and fried bananas on Division Street. We haven't neglected "American" fare either, and there are plenty of barbequed ribs, juicy hamburgers, serve-yourself salad bars, and apple pie in between.

What we have tried to do is avoid the pre-measured, prepackaged blandness that passes for food in the franchises that are sprouting like neon dandelions throughout the city. Why eat under the golden arch on Milwaukee Avenue when there is made-from-scratch soup, flaky kolacky, and tender loving care at Michelle's across the street?

Many of "our" restaurants remain undiscovered by people from outside the neighborhood. Some are better known. While wonderfully, ethnically diverse, all offer great food at bargain prices. Complete dinners cost $4.50 or less, and in several places you can dine heartily for under $2.50. The majority are family-run, with the cooking taking precedence over the decor. They have a cozy, almost-like-home feel to them. Some are even better than home.

We've also included a splurge section, a small but diverse

group of more expensive restaurants to visit when you feel the urge to celebrate. These are places that stand out in terms of excellent food, unusual atmosphere, or both.

There are sections on lunches, Sunday brunches, and also a selection of our favorite places for snacks, street eats, and related goodies—gyros, Italian beef, corned beef, pizza, hamburgers, pastry, etc. We've included a catch-all section to take care of restaurants that were either late discoveries, on the budget borderline, or else are notable for only a few special dishes.

To avoid any special treatment, we didn't tell any of the restaurant owners what we were up to, and generally tried to be as inconspicuous as anyone copying a six-page menu under the table could be. This book naturally reflects our personal opinions, but we have tried to present a fair and honest evaluation. Our main criterion was, of course, the food: Did it taste good? Was a generous amount of loving attention and skill devoted to its preparation? Did it lift our spirits, linger fondly in our memory, and would we look forward to eating it again?

For each restaurant included, we have sought to emphasize the best dishes, and, if necessary, to point out the bummers. Keep in mind that restaurants may vary nightly in quality and service, especially the small, inexpensive ones. Also menus are apt to change, due to the cook's inclination or seasonal bargains at the market. All prices were checked at press time. However, given the current state of the economy, there is only one certainty—they are bound to go up rather than down.

What follows, then, is a guide to Chicago's best budget restaurants—and there are some great ones. Our special favorites are denoted by an *. We hope we've included many tasty mouthfuls.

Jill and Ron Rohde
Chicago, Illinois

# Budget

# Authors' Note

Liquor, or its absence, is noted in the following manner:

Full Bar: Restaurants that serve their own cocktails, beer, and wine.

B.Y.O.: No liquor service, but you are welcome to bring your own wine or beer.

No liquor: Abstain in these restaurants.

Also, the vast majority of our restaurants don't take credit cards. Luckily, they are inexpensive. In our "splurge" category, where you might need more cash than you care to tote in your pocket, we indicate which credit cards are accepted.

Reservations are not necessary, unless noted.

# Bratislava

2527 N. Clark
Phone: 348-6938
Parking: Street (difficult)
Full bar

Wed.-Sat., 5:00 P.M.—10:00 P.M.
Sun., 5:00 P.M.—9:00 P.M.

The Bratislava has charm, one of Chicago's most unique waiters, and excellent food. However, it's a little hard to squeeze a complete meal under the $4.50 budget. The best bet is to come between 5:00 and 6:30 P.M. (Wednesday, Thursday, or Friday) when a dinner, including soup and salad, can be had for $3.50. Otherwise plan to spend a little extra—it's worth it.

Though the place has grown from a tiny one-room storefront (where you often had to double up at the table with another couple) to two rooms complete with bar, not much of the original flavor has been lost. There's still a large black and white aerial photo of Bratislava, white billowing curtains, colorful print tablecloths, and John, the headwaiter who never forgets a face. He'll probably cajole you into ordering an extra dish or two, and you won't regret it.

It's all hearty Czech cooking, featuring a crisp, meaty roast duck served with piquant red cabbage and bread-like dumpling ($3.75) as well as a selection of goulashes and paprikashes. Veal paprikash ($3.75) is excellent and boasts a beautifully seasoned gravy, but the beef goulash tastes monotonous and lacks subtlety. The sweet and sour stuffed cabbage ($3.25) has a creamy, dill-flavored sauce, and there are several roast beef dinners, including one served with lingonberries and another prepared Bratislava style, smothered in a sauce of celery, carrots, and finely diced pickles. For something deliciously different, try the plum dumplings topped with poppyseed sauce ($2.75 for five dumplings.)

For a starter we recommend the seven-vegetable salad (75¢), a spritely shredded slaw which blends perfectly with its accompanying pitcher of sour cream. Sauerkraut soup (65¢), if available, is nicely sour and unusually well seasoned.

The desserts are worth whatever room you can reserve for them, as both the apple and cheese strudels (75¢ each) are among the best around. For chocolate addicts, there's a rich, banana-studded, whipped cream concoction ladeled with homemade chocolate sauce (65¢).

# *Little Czechoslovakia

2609 S. Lawndale
Phone: 762-4968
Parking: Street
B.Y.O.

Tues.-Sun., 11:00 A.M.—8:00 P.M.
Closed Monday

We love Little Czechoslovakia. Not only does it serve Dick Butkus-sized portions at George Halas prices, but also exudes one of the warmest atmospheres around. Marta, its owner and cook, should be everyone's grandmother. She'll call out from the kitchen to see if you want more dumplings or gravy, and hug you if you clean your plate. People feel so much at home that the last time we were there one customer fell asleep at the table, snoring loudly.

The prices go easy on your earnings. Very few meals cost more than $2.50, including rye bread and homemade soup. Try either the liver dumpling or egg drop, if available, both of which have a base of rich chicken broth. Meat choices vary each day. There's usually szegedin goulash, tender roast pork, smoked butt, and roast chicken. On weekends Marta serves one of the best bargains in town: a moist, crisp, meaty roast duck for only $2.95. It's absolutely delicious. On Sundays, you can generally count on swiss steak with a sour cream-dill seasoned gravy. Two huge dumplings and a most genial sauerkraut share the plate with the meats.

The dining room, with its institutional green walls, isn't big on frills though it's roomy and neat. Classical music usually plays on the new FM radio. Fellow diners are primarily people from the neighborhood, though everyone is treated like an old friend. It's a restaurant one shouldn't miss.

Plan on an early dinner, as Marta occasionally runs out of some entrees.

# Olympic Restaurant

6139 W. Cermak, Cicero
Phone: 652-0101
Parking: Street
Full bar

Daily, 11:00 A.M.—8:00 P.M.
Closed Tuesday

With its carpeting, panelling, chandeliers, and bar, the Olympic looks fancier than other budget Bohemian restaurants. But there's no need to worry about fancy prices. Everything, other than steak, is under $3.00—which is really quite a bargain as dinners include soup, salad and dessert.

The daily offerings feature the usual beef, pork, and fowl. Their duck is as delicious as you would anticipate—moist, fleshy, crisp-skinned, and the $2.90 price never fails to amaze. Roast chicken ($2.90) is equally pleasing, especially since it comes with a tasty bread dressing. Roast pork ($2.80), breaded pork tenderloin ($2.80), and pickled beef ($3.00) are other choices. We found only the boiled beef ($2.80) disappointing. Its dill gravy sounded intriguing, but not only was it too thick and floury, there was also far too much of it.

Thursday's a good time to make it out to the Olympic as a host of specials is added to the menu. There are veal hearts with sour cream gravy ($2.00), pot roast and crisp potato pancakes ($2.80), meat loaf ($2.00), flicky (a ham-noodle combination, $2.10), and sometimes even rabbit ($3.00).

As for the meal's accessories, soups, in particular, are delicious. The vegetable soup is thick with white beans, barley, and noodles, the tripe soup is rich and peppery, and a light pleasant taste characterizes the beef noodle. Sliced bread dumplings, which accompany most of the meat dishes, are fairly light and interestingly textured. They are the only ones we've had in which you can actually see chunks of bread. Both the sweet and sour cabbage and the sauerkraut have a gentle tang.

The Olympic is quiet and sedate. People here seem to be "dining out" rather than just "eating out". The motherly waitresses really take care of you and add a nice, friendly touch.

# *Plaza Dining Room

7018½ Cermak, Berwyn
Phone: 484-9743
Parking: Street or shopping center lot
B.Y.O.

Daily, 10:30 A.M.—8:00 P.M.
Sun., 10:30 A.M.—7:00 P.M.

Located across from a sprawling shopping center and hidden between signs touting Liberty Loans and State Farm Insurance is the tiny Plaza Dining Room, a tribute to the way things used to be. The homey, old fashioned white ruffled curtains are the first sign that there's more to the place than just the food. The restaurant has a genuinely warm feel and, in fact, we've never had more attention showered upon us or our shoulders patted so often. The eight tables are packed, especially at noon, making it natural and necessary for people to share them, European-style.

Besides the evident good vibes, the food is great and the prices are low. Everything is homemade and a complete meal (with soup and dessert) costs $3.00 and under.

If you like fruit dumplings, try to make it out to the Plaza on Tuesday or Friday. Last time we were served four light, chewy, tennis ball-sized dumplings—two filled with apricots and two filled with plums ($2.30, including soup and dessert). Tart pot cheese, sugar, and melted butter make a fine contrasting topping.

The Plaza's most popular selection is the duck ($3.00). It's cooked to perfection—golden-crisp, tender, and meaty. Roast chicken with dressing ($2.80) is also tasty, as are the beef goulash ($2.80), thick-sliced roast pork ($2.80), and cabbage stuffed with a mixture of savory spiced ground meat ($2.30). Breaded pork tenderloin ($2.80), roast beef ($2.80), meat loaf ($2.00), liver ($2.80), and thuringer ($2.00) round out the menu.

Soups are substantial, especially the thick chicken giblet and delicate beef noodle. The bread dumplings are a little heavy, but the sauerkraut is just right. If you have any space left, there are usually prune, apricot, or cheese kolacky or poppyseed cake.

# Ridgeland Restaurant

6408 W. Cermak, Berwyn
Phone: 759-1151
Parking: Street
B.Y.O.

Daily, 11 A.M.—7:30 P.M.
Sat., 11 A.M.—5 P.M.
Closed Sunday

Yet another Bohemian bargain on Cermak Road, the Ridgeland is right up there with the best. It's a big, gleaming storefront that can be recognized by apricot-colored curtains, green awning, and proximity to the Berwyn Movie Theater.

The offerings are "standard Bohemian restaurant," meaning hearty, uncomplicated meat and dumplings. Don't be confused by the three prices on the menu. They stand for "small portion," "regular portion," and "business lunch" (the same size, but 35¢ to 40¢ cheaper than the "regular" and served only between 11 A.M. and 2 P.M.).

The Ridgeland's highlight is, of course, the $2.80 duck dinner. The meat is super juicy, though sometimes slightly fatty, and the skin is crackly crisp. Other good choices are roast pork ($2.70), meat loaf ($2.00), ribs with sauerkraut ($2.60) and, if available, beef with a sour cream-dill gravy ($2.60). All of the meats, except the latter, are covered with a light, savory brown gravy which enhances rather than drowns out the flavor.

The accompanying bread dumplings are the lightest and airiest we've tasted, and the sauerkraut is just sour enough. Soups are excellent, particularly the rich, flavorful eggdrop (similar to chicken-dumpling).

As for desserts, if you visit the Ridgeland on Friday, its fruit dumpling day and you're in for a treat. They're wondrous things, plump and mildly sweet. The pot cheese, butter, cinnamon-sugar topping provide a pungent contrast to the mild dumpling. Split an order ($1.90) among two to four people.

As with other Bohemian restaurants, the Ridgeland closes and runs out of certain dishes early. You can call up ahead of time to reserve the selection you want (particularly if you're counting on duck.)

# Stehlik's

4209 W. 26th
Phone: 762-3585
Parking: Street
No liquor

Daily, 11 A.M.—7:30 P.M.

If Archie Bunker lived in Chicago, Stehlik's would be his kind of restaurant. It's a small, homey, meat-and-potatoes place frequented primarily by people from this old Bohemian neighborhood. Most of the clientele are over forty, and lively conversation moves from counter to table and back again. As an outsider, you'll be looked over a bit but not enough to make you feel uncomfortable.

The food at Stehlik's is good, plentiful, and cheap. All meals include a meat course, vegetable, dumpling or potato, rye bread, and coffee. These complete meals average $2.00. A bowl of homemade soup is only 15¢ extra.

Simple, hearty foods make up the menu. There are short ribs ($2.40), roast pork ($2.00), meat loaf ($1.60), and bratwurst ($1.60). Roast chicken, though a little dry, comes with a good spicy bread dressing. Combine your meat with dumplings and either sweet-and-sour white cabbage or a sauerkraut mild enough to convert an avowed sauerkraut-hater.

The robust soup puts Campbell's to shame. There might be a thick beef goulash soup, a light, sweet beef noodle or a creamy cauliflower sporting big chunks of the vegetable. If you still have room for dessert, a choice of prune, pineapple, apricot, poppyseed, or cheese-filled kolackys cost 15¢ extra.

The decor is simple and pleasant with red-checked tablecloths and print wallpaper. Be sure to plan on an early dinner, as the restaurant closes at 7:30.

# Atlantic Fish & Chip

7115 W. Grand
Phone: 622-3259
Parking: Street
Full bar

Mon.-Thur., 4 P.M.—Midnight
Fri.-Sat., 4 P.M.—1:30 P.M.
Sun., 11 A.M.—Midnight
Reservations
Friday & Saturday

If you've always thought British food to be bland and boiled, check out the Atlantic Fish & Chip Restaurant. Only the cornbeef is boiled, and everything is well-seasoned. The menu features specialties from Wales, Scotland, and Ireland, as well as England, with several budget entrees for each category. House specialties include Welsh beef stew ($2.45), several meat pies (around $3.25), flaky pasties (meat-filled turnovers, $2.50), some great fish and chips ($2.50), and everyone's favorite, black pudding (similar to blood sausage.) A good choice is shepherds pie ($3.50), a nicely flavored chopped steak topped with mashed potatoes and melted cheese. All meals come with buttered Irish soda bread, usually chips (french fries), and the inevitable canned peas.

Desserts include trifle (a jam-filled, whipped cream and sherry-doused cake), rice pudding, and chocolate eclairs, each for 50¢. There is also a good blueberry tart, served with homemade custard sauce (75¢).

To wash everything down, Atlantic has an extensive supply of English, Irish, Scottish and Welsh ales, beers, and stouts. A limited and fairly inexpensive wine list also bears perusing.

The Atlantic's owners, Emyr and Mair Morris, who are from Wales, have decorated their long dining room to resemble a lavish British pub. There's red flocked wall paper, black beams, and heavy chandeliers. On weekends, folksingers entertain, and the place takes on a lively, spirited air.

# St. Andrews Fish & Chips

4542 N. Western
Phone: 784-6200
Parking: Street
B.Y.O.

Daily, 4 P.M.—10 P.M.
Fri.-Sat., 4 P.M.—11 P.M.
Closed Monday

St. Andrews Fish and Chips is the only Scottish restaurant we know of in Chicago. Fortunately, it's a good one. The tiny storefront is both tidy and cheerful. Walls are papered in tartan plaids and further decorated with pictures of the Scottish countryside, soldiers in full dress, and coats of arms.

The compact menu offers Scottish and English specialties, primarily fish dishes or offsprings of the meat pie and pastie. Everything is well prepared, neatly served, and tastily homemade. Dinners include bread or rolls, chips (french fries), and canned vegetables, and several cost under $2.00.

Their fish and chips ($1.95) should keep you out of the franchise outfits. The fish is dipped in a special batter, then quick-fried until golden puffy outside, moist and flaky inside. It tastes fantastic, especially when sprinkled with a few drops of malt vinegar. Scallops ($2.95) and shrimp ($3.10) are two other deep-fried offerings. The salmon croquettes ($1.95) are delicious when feather-light, but at times have been gluey. Baked halibut or sole ($2.95) are appealingly served in a melted butter sauce and are both quite good.

For non-fish fanciers, one of the better selections is the Cornish pastie ($1.95), a savory mixture of well-seasoned ground chuck, chopped potatoes, and carrots wrapped in a rich flaky crust. Forfar bridie ($1.95) is a close relative but the ground meat is more strongly seasoned and the crust even crisper. Scotch pie, a similar pastry-meat combination ($1.95), steak and kidney pie ($3.15), or a pastry-enclosed sausage roll ($1.95) are other tasty options.

Portions at St. Andrews are not enormous, so if it's been a long time between meals, try ordering an a la carte side dish in addition to the regular dinner. Practically everything on the menu (meat pie, croquettes, etc.) is available on the side for 95¢. Dessert, too, is extra, but the creamy rice pudding (50¢) has a smooth mellow taste, and the sherry trifle (55¢) is served with mounds of whipped cream.

Anything on the menu can be ordered to take out at considerably lower prices.

# Ding Hoe

105 W. Division
Phone: 944-8433
Parking: Street
B.Y.O.

Daily, 4 P.M.—11:30 P.M.
Closed Tuesday

For many years Ding Hoe was a bleak little hole in the wall on Clark Street that enjoyed a devoted following for its fine low-priced food. Since it moved around the corner, the food is still fine, and the place bigger and somewhat less drab. The menu is filled with over a hundred entrees, and not many Cantonese favorites are left out. Portions are quite generous, and prices are reasonable.

Everyone seems to begin their meal with egg rolls ($1.20), as Ding Hoe does them fine. The crackly shells are stuffed with crisp vegetables, shrimp, and pork. Fried won ton ($1.00) is also delicious. Vegetable soup (50¢) is a flavorful, nourishing broth filled with sliced fresh mushrooms, Chinese greens, pork, and tomatoes.

Choosing an entree calls for some heavy decision-making. Our favorite dish is kai ding ($3.25), a well-seasoned blend of chicken, black and button mushrooms, peapods, water chestnuts, and almonds. Not far behind are shrimp in lobster sauce ($2.85) and steamed beef with mushrooms, waterchestnuts, and peapods ($2.50). Buck toy tenderloin steak ($3.65) features tender beef and greens done up in oyster sauce, and a less expensive but just as tasty variation, buck toy cha shu ($2.85), substitutes barbequed pork for the steak. The sweet and sour dishes (pork, $2.55; chicken, $3.40) maintain their crispness and include an ample portion of meat. Fried rice ($1.70) is moist, and beef-mushroom chop suey ($2.45) is quite good, but the chow mein falls flat, primarily because the noodles are soggy. (They should switch to the super-thin, crisp ones.)

Service at Ding Hoe is prompt and courteous, and you are never hurried. There is generally seating as the restaurant is roomy. We think it's one of the best budget places to eat in the Division/Rush Street area.

# Golden Crown

1951 Cherry Lane,
Northbrook
Phone: 272-1812
Parking: Lot
B.Y.O.

Daily, 11:00 A.M.—8:30 P.M.
Sunday, 4:00 P.M.—8:30 P.M.

For some excellent Chinese food in the northern suburbs, try the Golden Crown. The outstanding feature of this restaurant is owner Ray Wong's obvious emphasis on quality. He relies on crisp fresh ingredients and uses plenty of them. If the menu states that a dish will have peapods and almonds, you don't have to conduct a search party. There are well over sixty main dishes on the menu. Almost all cost between $1.75 and $2.85. Another 95¢ will bring a dinner complete with soup, fried wonton, egg roll, fried rice, dessert, and tea!

Some entrees worth a try are the breast of chicken sub gum chow mein ($2.75), the sweet-and-sour pork with man-
latter is an interesting blend of barbequed pork, peapods, water chestnuts, scrambled egg, and thin transparent noodles.

*CHINESE*

darin oranges ($2.75), and the char su sai foon ($2.85). The Lichee nuts, candied ginger, and pineapple are included in the exotic sweet and sour beef ($2.75). Other possibilities are the breaded hong sue shrimp ($2.15) or the hong sue chicken kow with black mushrooms ($3.05).

For appetizers, the fried wonton ($1.05) and egg rolls ($1.15) are crisp and fresh-tasting. The meaty barbequed ribs ($2.05) sport a thick, gooey sauce but can occasionally be tough. They also make one of the best won ton soups we've ever tasted.

The setting at Golden Crown is an easy blend of oriental and modern. There are two medium-sized dining rooms which provide comfortable seating. The pace is relaxed, but be sure to plan on an early dinner as the restaurant closes at 8:30.

Directions: Take Edens Expressway north to Dundee. West on Dundee to Waukegan Road. South to Schermer, then turn west to first stoplight. Turn left into shopping center and look for Golden Crown.

# New China

3710 W. Dempster, Skokie
Phone: 674-3426
Parking: Lot, in front
B.Y.O.

Daily, 11:00 A.M.—9:00 P.M.
Sat., 11:00 A.M.—11:00 P.M.

Good Cantonese restaurants are always in demand, and since undergoing new management, New China helps meet the call. Though you can easily go over the $4.50 per person budget here, portions are mountainous. Most chow mein and chop suey dishes cost under $3.00, while the more interesting specialties (other than higher-priced steak and lobster dishes) average about $3.60. It's definitely best to come here with a group and share several dishes.

Start with egg roll ($1.30). It's crisp, not oily, and loaded with crunchy vegetables. Among the entrees we particularly like are the shrimps in black bean sauce ($3.75), the chicken subgum chow mein Cantonese style ($3.35), and the beef kow ($3.85), a savory combination of beef, peapods, green beans, water chestnuts, and mushrooms in an oyster sauce. The young chew won ton ($3.65) is unusual and delicious. The won ton maintain their crunch in a sauce brimming with chicken, shrimp, beef, cashews, and vegetables. Our special favorite is the fun shee ($3.15), thin, cellophane noodles, sauteed with good-sized shrimp, pork, chewy black mushrooms, crisp peapods, sprouts, and water chestnuts. The sweet-and-sour dishes are just average.

Service at New China is attentive without being overbearing. Our teapot was refilled quickly before we even had time to ask.

It's best to arrive by at least 8:00. The waiters start eating at around 8:30, and most are dressed for home at around 9:00. Also special lunches are served from 11:30 to 3:30, which include soup and one entree, priced from $1.85 to $2.35.

# Orchid Room

5951 N. Broadway
Phone: 878-1155
Parking: Street
B.Y.O.

Mon.-Thur., 11:30 A.M.—10:00 P.M.
Fri.-Sat., 11:30 A.M.—11:30 P.M.
Sun., Noon—10:00 P.M.

At last! A good Mandarin restaurant that's not in the splurge category. No dish on the menu is over $4.95, and most are under $3.00. Yet an impressive variety of popular northern offerings are available.

Be sure to start your meal with a soup and/or appetizer. Shrimp toast ($1.00) is a worthy beginning, even though its quality varies. When it's good, it's very, very good—crisp and buttery tasting. Steamer bo-bo ($1.45) are delicate meat-filled dumplings, but are so tiny that you're liable to ask, "Is that all there is?" Kwo-teh (fried pork-filled dumplings, $1.25) and fried won ton ($1.00) are both quite good.

Hot and sour soup (60¢) lives up to its name. The thick, well-seasoned broth is filled with egg, tree-fungus and scallions, and has a pleasant, warming after-bite. Sizzling rice soup ($1.75 or $1.95) serves 2 or 3 and is a mildly peppery broth containing snowpeas, waterchestnuts, black and button mushrooms, and either chicken or shrimp into which are dropped crisp rice cakes that literally do snap, crackle, and pop.

Some main dishes are chicken with cashews ($2.95), Mongolian beef (a glazed combination of thin beef slices, scallions, and hot pepper, $2.95), and beef with seasonal vegetables ($2.75). Moo shu pork ($2.50), which is generally our favorite Mandarin dish, lives up to expectations. Razor-thin pancakes are accompanied by a crunchy mixture of finely shredded pork, scallions, bamboo shoots, and egg. An unusual and excellent dish is crab meat soong ($3.95), a delicate blending of thin crisp noodles, minced crab, scallions, carrots, and waterchestnuts, also served with pancakes.

Finish your meal with glazed apples or bananas ($1.60 for six pieces), as sensuous a dessert as there is. Working at your table, the waitress dips the hot syrup-coated fruit into ice water until the coating reaches a brittle candly-like hardness. It's sticky, sweet and delightful, only to be avoided if you've recently visited the dentist.

# *Wing Yee's

2556 N. Clark
Phone: 935-7380
Parking: Street (difficult)
B.Y.O.

Daily, 3:00 P.M.—11:00 P.M.
Closed Monday

Although it has slipped a notch from its past glory, Wing Yee's remains our favorite place for Cantonese food. We have yet to taste better sweet and sour pork, pressed duck, or egg foo young. Soups are superb too, particularly the vegetable (70¢), a light broth filled with fresh mushrooms, spinach, tomatoes, celery, pork, etc.

Among the main dishes, several are recommended. All feature quality ingredients, are served hot and taste fresh. The almond-topped pressed duck ($3.10) is brilliant—a perfect contrast of crisp greaseless skin and juicy meat. The sweet and sour pork or ribs ($2.70) have a light crisp coating and come in a delicious gooey sauce. Chicken subgum chow mein Cantonese style ($3.10) is excellent—a bounty of crunchy fresh vegetables, white meat, almonds, and pan-fried noodles. A more unusual but equally delicious dish is sai foon ($2.90), a blend of glossy transparent noodles, pork, shrimp, and scallions in a soy-molasses sauce. Its cousin, chow foon ($2.20), is crisper, heavy on the bean sprouts, and equally good. Beef and vegetable dishes (beef and broccoli, beef and green beans, etc.) are also done up right, as is the moist, well-seasoned pork fried rice ($1.80).

Service at Wing Yee's can be slow, though Ronnie's table-clearing prowess is legendary. The wait for a table used to be long enough to get well into *War and Peace,* but lately the Classic Comic version is about all you'll have time for. Whatever the wait, we feel it's worth it.

# Liborio

4005 N. Broadway
Phone: 549-8723
Parking: Street
Full bar

Mon.-Fri. & Sun., 11:00 A.M. —Midnight
Sat., 11:00 A.M.—2:00 A.M.

Liborio has something of the flavor of old Havana mixed in with present-day Chicago. The dining room is spacious and modern—a blend of Latin, early American, and western frontier. Cuban businessmen pore over their papers, attractive young couples dine here along with a suave-looking man or two who would be perfect for casting in a remake of Boston Blackie. It all makes for an interesting atmosphere, especially at night, when an elaborately coiffured blond unexpectedly begins a medley of show tunes on the piano.

The menu, comprised of several Cuban specialties, is fascinating in its own right. There's the traditional arroz con pollo (chicken and rice, $2.50), a relatively inexpensive paella ($4.00; call in ahead of time to order), and a delicious, thick black bean soup. Sweet, sauteed ripe plantains (bananas) or deep-fried plantain chips (75¢) make excellent appetizers.

There are a dozen dinner possibilities which average $3.00 and include a basket of hot crusty french bread, salad, rice, usually a soup, and coffee. The roast chicken, Cuban-style ($2.95), is served with a light tomato sauce, rice and black bean soup, which tastes delicious ladled over the rice. The lightly sauteed pork cutlet and the tender, marinated carne asada (roast beef) are both well prepared. There are also several interesting, inexpensive seafood dishes.

The menu features no less than fifteen egg dishes. The unusual ripe plantain omelette ($1.50) tastes slightly sweet. There is also a selection of Cuban sandwiches and several desserts including refreshing guava or papaya with cream cheese, bread pudding, an excellent flan (60¢), and an even better creamy pudding called natilla (50¢).

# El Saz Taqueria

3238 W. Fullerton
Phone: 384-9043
Parking: Street
B.Y.O.

Daily, 10:00 A.M.—10:00 P.M.

The big sign over the door reads "un rinconcito de Cuba" (a little corner of Cuba), the one painted on the window says "El Saz Taqueria", and the menu touts a "Zas taco". Whatever you call it, the restaurant looks just like countless other taco joints throughout the city. But it ain't. El Saz prepares some excellent Cuban home-cooked meals, all under $2.75. Seven dinners are listed on the menu, and one daily special is chalked up on a blackboard. Dinners range from roast pork to fried kingfish; most are served with salad, French bread, moros, cristianos (blackbeans and rice), and, sometimes, fried bananas.

The boliche asado (Cuban roast beef, $2.35) is a fine dinner to try. The tender, juicy beef is covered with peppers, onions, and a gentle tomato sauce. Mashed dry meat ($2.50), on the other hand, may not be for everyone. The slightly salty shredded beef is stewed in tomato sauce along with peppers, onions, and cabbage.

Daily specials *are* generally special. We've had an excellent pollo guisado (chicken stew, $2.50) and outstanding cola de res (oxtail stew, $2.75), as tender and flavorful as any we've ever eaten. The oxtail stew comes with some delicate, slightly sweet, fried platanos (bananas) and slices of lime.

El Saz offers a variety of tostadas, burritos, and tacos. (Try the Zas taco.) It's also a good place to sample a Cuban sandwich ($1.00)—usually ham, pork, and cheese fitted between French bread and pressed hot and toasty on a grill. For drinking, the batidos (frothy blenderized drinks made from milk, ice, and tropical fruit) are delicious. There's also a nice natilla for dessert (25¢ or 50¢).

An exceptionally friendly, homey place, though language can be a slight hassle.—Further confusion: EL SAZ is now *LA ESTRELLA ORIENTAL*. Same menu plus additional Chinese section. New phone: 278-5445.—

# Café Bernard

2100 N. Halsted
Phone: 871-2100
Parking: Street
Full bar

Lunch: Tues.-Fri., 11:00 A.M.—2:00 P.M.
Dinner: Daily, 5:00 P.M.—11:00 P.M.
Closed Monday

Café Bernard offers a cozy setting for some generally well prepared, reasonably priced French food. Although French restaurants never come under a strictly budget category, at Café Bernard it is possible to dine on entree, salad, and bread for around $4.00. Soup and dessert are a la carte.

All meals begin with a basket of French bread and fresh greens tossed with a tart mustardy dressing. The entrees, written on a blackboard, vary each day but always include meat, fish, and fowl selections. There are several popular standards represented as well as a few more creative dishes.

Chicken Nicoise ($3.95) is definitely worth a try. Tender sauteed chicken is topped by a colorful zucchini-eggplant-onion-studded tomato sauce. Duck ($4.50) is a well-prepared, large portion with crisp skin and subtle orange sauce. Trout almondine ($4.20) is tender and flaky, but we found sole Veronique ($3.95) to be soggy and tasteless. Lamb stew ($3.95) and boeuf bourguignon ($3.95) are served up in huge bowls and make for hearty peasant fare. The accompanying vegetables vary in skill of preparation, with the most successful being the hot ratatouille.

Averaging $1.00, dessert choices might include a cold smooth creme caramel, a rather ordinary apple tarte, or a wedge of camembert served with fruit and crackers.

The dining area at Café Bernard offers a prime example of how a plain corner storefront can be transformed into an intimate bistro. Natural pine-panelled walls, hanging funnel lamps, checked tablecloths, and lined drawings of cooking utensils help create the mood. One drawback is that when the restaurant is crowded the noise approaches sonic boom level, and the seating ranges between cramped and claustrophobic.

# *La Crêperie

2845 N. Clark
Phone: 528-9050
Parking: Street (difficult)
B.Y.O.

Daily, 5:00 P.M.—11:00 P.M.
Closed Tuesday
No reservations accepted

Dining at La Crêperie is always enjoyable. The food is delicious and the price pleasingly low. Crêpes range from 40¢ for a plain crêpe with butter up to $3.25 for a seafood crêpe. Most cost well under $2.00. The restaurant is small, cozy and tastefully decorated. The young owner hails from Brittany, home of the crêpe. He's always busy at the griddle turning out crêpes with amazing speed.

The chalked up menu features 12 buckwheat dinner crêpes. The chicken crêpe ($2.15) is remarkably soothing—large pieces of white meat in a delicate cream sauce garnished with parmesan-sprinkled, sauteed mushrooms. Another favorite is the ham, cheese and tomato crêpe ($1.75). The flavors blend nicely and come out something like a mild pizza. The ham and cheese ($1.35) and ham and egg ($1.35) are variations on the same theme. Both are tasty as is the spinach creme crêpe ($1.25).

The crêpes, folded envelope style, are not tea-room size. One, along with a dessert crêpe or salad (75¢) makes a meal. The crouton and parmesan-topped tossed greens are fresh and the dressing, tart and flavorful.

The whole wheat dessert crêpes are almost more pleasure than the dinner crêpes. The crêpe with jam (70¢) is a melting mouthful and the banana, strawberry, or apple whipped cream crêpes ($1.40, each) contain a fresh fruit filling and are topped with whipped cream and powdered sugar.

An appealing bargain, if you'd like a taste of everything, is the chicken crêpe dinner. The $3.70 price includes a dinner crêpe, salad, dessert crêpe, and beverage. Most people bring their own wine, but the hot cider mulled with cinnamon sticks is delicious and tranquilizing.

Expect a wait at La Crêperie as seating is limited, and there's always a patiently waiting crowd.

# *The French Kitchen

3437 W. 63rd
Phone: 778-9476
Parking: Street
B.Y.O.

Daily, 5:00 P.M.—11:00 P.M.
Sun., Noon—10:00 P.M.
Closed Monday

The French Kitchen is like an oasis in a neighborhood not particularly noted for its gourmet dining spots. It is also, in our opinion, the best low-priced French restaurant in Chicago. It is run by Lorraine Hooker, who, armed with French cooking lessons but no previous restaurant experience, decided to open up her own place. Working on a shoestring budget, she and her kids turned an empty storefront into a charming replica of a French country inn replete with lush hanging plants, colorful print tablecloths, and a beamed ceiling.

The menu features five regular entrees and two daily specials. Most are priced at $4.00 and include a salad tossed with a good basil-tarragon-flavored vinaigrette dressing, rice, French bread, and beverage. Sometimes included is a complimentary appetizer of deep-fried, melt-in-your-mouth mashed potato puffs.

The five main entrees are a classic coq au vin, ham en croute (baked in a pastry crust), beef Wellington ($6.30), a meltingly tender sole, garnished with mushrooms and shrimp and baked in a paper sack ($4.95), and a marvelous chicken marengo in a delicate tomato sauce graced with fresh whole mushrooms. Also noteworthy are the creatively prepared daily specials. Estouffade is a delicate French country stew which blends fork-tender beef, onions, potatoes, and green olives. The unusual citriade combines sole and scallops in a light wine sauce, subtly flavored with orange peel. Chicken stew with sweet carrots, fresh mushrooms, and whole new potatoes, or fresh trout stuffed with chopped spinach, mushrooms, tomatoes, and tiny shrimp are also scrumptious.

Soups, appetizers and desserts are a la carte. Onion soup (65¢) is a regular and the du jour offerings (50¢) can include oxtail and beef-barley. We particularly recommend closing your meal with either the poached fresh pear lavished in a brandy whipped cream sauce (75¢) or the rich, creamy chocolate mousse (75¢). The bread pudding with whiskey sauce (75¢) could use a touch more spirit.

# Berghoff

17 W. Adams
Phone: 427-3170
Parking: Impossible
Full bar

Daily, 11:00 A.M.—9:00 P.M.
Closed Sunday

Berghoff has everything: good food, varied menu, comfortable setting (provided you're not rushed), serious waiters, and maybe even a famous face or two, especially if they're being indicted. (Berghoff is next door to the Federal Building.) While it's not the only good budget restaurant downtown, it is the best.

The menu varies daily and tilts toward the German. There's wiener schnitzel ($3.45), kassler ribchen (smoked young pork loin, $3.40), sauerbraten ($3.25), roulade of beef ($3.40), and Alpen ragout, a savory blend of veal slices and fresh mushrooms in wine sauce ($3.25). In addition, there's a very interesting selection of fish and seafood, including fresh Boston scrod ($3.30), broiled white fish ($4.00), fried oysters ($3.10), and a great combination that features a small lobster tail as well as sole, shrimp, and scallops ($4.20). There's also an ample sampling of steaks and chops.

Most dinners, other than steaks, run under $3.50 and include a really good rye bread and two side dishes, perhaps German fried potatoes, spaetzel, creamed spinach, glazed carrots, or fresh corn on the cob. Dessert, soup, and beverage are extra. Soups (45¢) are generally delicious and run the gamut from cream of asparagus to oxtail. In summer there's a lovely cold fruit soup filled with strawberries and cherries. Standouts among desserts are lemon meringue pie (55¢), German chocolate cake (55¢), and a delicate moist crunch cake (45¢).

# Hogen's

4560 N. Lincoln
Phone: 334-9406
Parking: Lot
Full bar

Daily, 11:00 A.M.—1:00 A.M.
Sun., Noon—1:00 A.M.

Hogen's was selected by some Hollywood producers as the archtypical Polish neighborhood restaurant-bar, and was used as the setting for a Polish "Walton Family" TV pilot, titled "Mama Kovack." This has caused a few chuckles at Hogen's, which is actually your typical German neighborhood restaurant-bar, a fixture at Wilson and Lincoln since 1890.

However, one thing at Hogen's stands out as hardly typical—the prices. It is easily the cheapest German restaurant we've found. You have to look hard to find anything over $3.00 on the menu, which rotates daily. Six to ten entrees are featured, with roast pork ($2.50), roast beef ($2.50), and bratwurst ($2.25) being everyday standbys.

Weekends are your best bet, as the menu is the fullest and the choices are most traditionally German. On Saturdays, there's sauerbraten and dumplings ($2.50), beef rouladen ($2.50), smoked butt and red cabbage ($2.50), and the most inexpensive roast duck ($2.75) we've found this side of Cicero. Sunday features more of the same plus a bargain-priced wiener schnitzel ($2.50). On weekdays, the moist meatloaf ($1.85) on Monday is a good bet as are the braised oxtails ($2.10) on Thursdays. On all dishes, ask them to go easy on the gravy. All entrees come with two side dishes (try for the red cabbage) plus rye bread.

Portions will fill you, especially if you begin a meal with homemade soup (40¢). The pea soup on Monday is exceptionally well-made. Dessert's available too, for an extra tab. The strudel's tasty (50¢), but we suggest avoiding the cardboard-like crusted pies.

Hogen's dining patrons sit in a panelled backroom, secluded by a partition from the rowdier drinkers in the bar up front. Everything about the place—food, patrons, and people who work there—seems hearty and robust.

# *Schwaben Stube

3500 N. Lincoln
Phone: 348-8856
348-8891
Parking: Street
Full bar

Tues.-Sun., 11:30 A.M.—Midnight
Fri.-Sat., 11:30 A.M.—1:00 A.M.
Closed Monday

Finding a good but inexpensive German restaurant is as hard as finding a Cub fan at White Sox Park. We think the Schwaben Stube does an admirable job of filling you and not the check. Complete dinners are generally under $5.00, but you can find several intriguing selections for under $4.00. Meals are hearty and include appetizer or soup, salad, entree, side dishes, dessert, and beverage.

Some of the more interesting specials for under $4.00 are beef stroganoff with noodles, roast pork loin and applesauce, roulade of beef (rolled beef with a bacon-onion-herb stuffing) with potato dumplings, breaded veal chops, red cabbage, and crisp German fried potatoes. The wiener schnitzel, sauerbraten with spaetzle, and Kassler ribs with red cabbage will run you $4.25 each.

For a starter try either the creamy herring or the robust lentil, liver dumpling, or pea soup. The salads are all tasty, especially the tangy marinated kidney beans or the cucumber. And that super, paper-thin pumpernickel goes with all! Desserts if you're able, range from apple strudel to Liederkranz cheese.

The atmosphere at Schwaben Stube is like a comfortable Bavarian inn. The front rooms, with their stained glass, painted murals, and checked tablecloths, are far more attractive and cozy. Also, on weekends you'll be better able to enjoy the music of a jolly violin-piano duo and a charmingly enthusiastic hostess who sporadically bursts into theatrical renditions of old German favorites.

The friendly, German-accented waitresses are helpful and efficient. Some have been at Schwaben Stube since it opened twenty-eight years ago. You have the feeling that many of the customers have been faithful that long as well.

# Aesop's Tables

2856 N. Broadway — Daily, 11:00 A.M.—2:00 A.M.
Phone: 528-7600
Parking: Street (difficult)
Full bar

Aesop's Tables captures the atmosphere of a Greek country inn, New Town style. The hanging wine jugs, beamed stucco ceiling and exposed brick walls lend a cozy atmosphere. Located on a stretch that has been overdosed with gyros stands, its food rivals that of the more fabled Greek eateries on Halsted and on Lawrence, and just about everything on their extensive menu is priced below $3.00.

The saganaki (flaming, brandy-doused cheese pie, $1.75) is served with enough flourish to delight a pyromaniac. The egg-lemon soup (35¢ or 50¢) is smooth and pleasantly tart-flavored.

In the entree category, moussaka (layered eggplant-ground lamb casserole topped by bechamel sauce, $2.50) is an eye as well as taste pleaser. The portion is generous and the flavors merge nicely. Pastitsio (macaroni-ground meat-cheese casserole, $2.25) is juicy and tastes freshly made. The braised lamb ($2.75) is unusually tender, and the combination plate ($3.45) includes some of the best of everything. Both fried squid ($2.25) and octopus in wine sauce ($2.25) are prepared with expertise, but the two chicken dishes are somewhat peaked.

The bar at Aesop's Tables can get kind of boisterous at times, occasionally to the glass-breaking point. Opaa!

# *Grecian Restaurant Psistaria

2412-14 W. Lawrence Daily, 11:30 A.M.—4:00 A.M.
Phone: 728-6308
Parking: Street
Full bar

The Grecian Psistaria reflects the Greek zest for living. A Greek electric combo plays lively tunes up front while casting lingering glances at tables of unescorted young women. Waiters burst into song at unexpected moments, and from time to time people are moved to dance. It's spirited, noisy and fun. The food also happens to be among the best Greek cooking in town.

The dining room is mammoth, with murals of Greek seaside villages and a grotto-like effect on one wall. Waiters, dressed in the traditional white shirt and black tie, refuse to neglect you. They fill your bread basket at least three times and your water glass, four. The menu is comprehensive, and most entrees cost $2.50 and under.

Try starting off your meal with a bowl of avgolemono, egg-lemon soup (50¢). It's smooth and nicely tart. The eggplant salad (75¢) is creamy and heavy with garlic. The huge portion of fish roe (85¢) is smooth-textured, not overly fishy and goes beautifully with the soft Greek bread.

The menu is weighted with baked or braised lamb dishes (average, $2.50), served with a side-dish of either cauliflower, green beans, eggplant, rice, or potatoes. The excellent moussaka ($2.15) is at least three inches high and features a potato layer in addition to the usual eggplant and ground meat. The dolmades (rolled grape leaves stuffed with ground lamb) are bathed in a tangy egg-lemon sauce, with just the slightest hint of mint. If you're after something more unusual, a well prepared octopus with macaroni (Fridays only, $2.25) and fried squid ($2.25) are available.

For dessert there is a wonderfully smooth creamy rice pudding (75¢) in addition to the usual pastries.

When the band plays, drinks go up astronomically; for instance, a $4.00 bottle of wine will cost you $7.00. There is no band on Mondays, so drinks are lower and the place is much quieter.

# Greek Islands

766 W. Jackson
Phone: 782-9855
Parking: Street
Full bar

Mon.-Thur., 11:30 A.M.—Midnight
Fri.-Sat., 11:30 A.M.—2:00 A.M.
Sun., Noon—Midnight

You could say that when you've eaten in one Greek restaurant you've eaten in them all. However, we've found subtle nuances to distinguish one Greek eatery from another. For instance, Greek Islands makes what has to be the best saganaki in town, their menu is more adventurous than most (snails, octopus in wine sauce, plus unusual daily specials,) and their waiters wear light blue jackets rather than the usual black and white outfit. Their prices, happily enough, are not distinguishable from any other Greek restaurant—they're the same good old cheap.

Reliable entrees include fresh tasting dolmades ($2.25), braised lamb with vegetables or rice ($2.75), and gyros ($2.50). The combination plate ($3.25) generally includes lamb, moussaka, dolmades, potatoes, rice, and vegetables as well as a sampling of one of the day's specials. There's also a nice variety of fish—fried smelts ($2.25), whole snapper and sea bass (prices fluctuate), and fried cod (bakalao) in garlic sauce.

From among the daily specials we favor lamb and artichokes with egg-lemon sauce ($3.10), stewed lima beans ($1.00) and shrimp Greek-style, which are served in their shell over rice in a light tomato-egg sauce ($3.25).

Soft, sesame-sprinkled Greek bread comes with each entree. An extra $1.50 buys a complete meal, which includes egg-lemon soup, a good-sized Greek salad, dessert, and coffee. Don't overlook the saganaki (flaming cheese). Each bite combines the lacy crispness of the coating with the incredibly rich melted cheese.

The interior of Greek Islands bears evidence of a visit by the mysterious muralist whose specialty seems to be creating bland turquoise seascapes on Greek restaurant walls. However, there's nothing dull about the atmosphere. It's lively and friendly.

# Mykonos' Windmill

6025 N. Lincoln
Phone: 262-3039
Parking: Lot
Full bar

Daily, 10:30 A.M.—3:00 A.M.

Mykonos' Windmill is easily the most attractive of our Greek restaurants. It is both subdued and sophisticated, with carpeting, white tablecloths, linen napkins, and a grillwork partition separating one dining room from the other. Due to the lighting and use of color, the interior seems bathed in a soft blue aura which is very soothing. The menu is slightly more expensive than some of the other Greek restaurants, though most of the entrees fall well within our budget. Except for an unusual flaming shrimp saganaki ($2.50), the menu is fairly standard.

There's a zesty, meat-filled moussaka ($2.50), dolmades ($2.50) with a milder than usual lemon-egg sauce, souvlaki ($3.85), and a crusty gyros ($2.45). There are the usual tender roast and braised lamb dishes as well as the more unusual fried smelts ($2.95), and some excellent, non-rubbery fried squid ($2.95).

Meals begin with a complimentary appetizer course featuring a delicious, mild fish roe, a pungent, garlicky yogurt-cucumber mixture, navy bean salad, and a butter-cheese spread.

Complete dinners are available for 75¢ to $1.50 extra. They include a Greek salad with a nice hunk of feta, coffee, and somewhat disappointing desserts.

Mykonos' is not the place to go for glass-breaking and merry-making, but rather for its serene atmosphere, generally well-prepared food, and fine service.

# Parthenon

314 S. Halsted — Daily, 11 A.M.—2:00 A.M.
Phone: 726-2407
Parking: Street, and a free lot (evenings only)
Full bar

The Parthenon is unquestionably Chicago's most popular Greek restaurant, though we don't feel the cuisine necessarily surpasses that of a number of other Greek eateries. The service is generally swift, and the waiters move about with considerable energy and grace. The two large dining rooms are usually filled to capacity.

The menu features several standout dishes, all very reasonably priced. The generous portion of saganaki ($1.35) is done up beautifully here and served with pizzazz. The gyros (grilled lamb and beef, $2.35) is perfectly prepared—thin-sliced and crusty. The sharp-flavored spinach pie is served in an unusually large portion. Roast leg of lamb is excellent, and the braised lamb ($2.50) is both mild-flavored and tender. Try your lamb with either stewed eggplant or zucchini.

The two casseroles fare less well. Moussaka tastes more like a heavily salted meat loaf than a subtly spiced lamb and eggplant combination. The meat seems to be hiding altogether in the noodle-dominated pastitsio.

Desserts, however, are expertly prepared. The fresh, flaky baklava lives up to its reputation, and the galactobouriko is smooth, mildly sweet and not too soggy. At 35¢, they are sold at a price more like that of a bakery than a restaurant.

# Guatemala Restaurant

1027 W. Wilson
Phone: 271-2761
Parking: Street
B.Y.O.

Daily, 11:00 A.M.—1:00 A.M.
Closed Tuesday

Next time you're hit by an uncontrollable craving for Guatemalan food, try the Guatemala restaurant on Wilson Avenue. Squeezed in between the Habana Barber Shop and an East Indian grocery on one of Chicago's livelier streets, the Guatemala is the place to go for food from south of the Mexican border.

It's a little family-run place that offers cuisine quite similar to Mexican. Posted on the wall, the brief menu is weighted with beef dishes, averaging $2.50. There's bistek with fried potatoes, beef with spicy ranchero sauce, and a very tender and flavorful carne guisada (beef stew), served with rice and beans. For contrast, try the large bowl of shrimp soup. Though it's priced somewhat high at $3.00, the tomato-based broth is tasty and loaded with shrimp.

Specials vary each day and might include chile rellenos, homemade tamales or sauteed pork chops. Excellent as a snack or light lunch are the refried beans, served with a side dish of sweet fried bananas ($1.25). A plateful of napkin-covered warm tortillas accompanies all meals.

Each table in the small, paneled restaurant is set with a lovely embroidered Guatemalan tablecloth. Service is friendly, though there may be a slight, but not insurmountable, language barrier. Food is made to order, the pace is relaxed, and the cook can often be heard singing in the kitchen.

# Bon Ton

1153 N. State
Phone: 943-0538
Parking: Street (difficult)
B.Y.O.

Daily, 11:00 A.M.—10:00 P.M.
Closed Sunday

Located in the midst of the Rush Street glitter, Bon Ton offers a welcome relief from the splashy tourist places that dominate the area. It has a genteel tea room aura that feels distinctly European. The food is beautifully served, the pastry is fabulous, and the prices a pleasant surprise. All entrees, including salad and bread, cost $3.50 or less. Service, however, tends to be abrupt and snooty.

The most popular selection on the brief menu is shish kebab (a half order, at $3.25, is ample). The meat is well marinated, plump and tender. Tons of rice pilaf accompany it. Chicken paprika ($3.25) is fork tender and tastes great with the buttery spaetzle that accompanies it. If you're a stuffed-pepper freak, Bon Ton has some of the tastiest we've ever eaten. The peppers are cooked until just tender and their flavor mixes smoothly with the ground meat filling and mild tomato sauce ($3.00). Stuffed cabbage ($3.00), Hungarian goulash ($3.25) and meat-filled bliny ($2.00) are three other interesting possibilities.

Share a piroshkee (50¢) to start off your meal. The peppery ground meat-filled pastry is superb. There are also several soups, the most tasty being the beef soup with won ton-like meat dumplings (70¢) or the bean with smoked meat and dumpling (40¢ a cup; 50¢ a bowl).

Try to save room for dessert or if you can't, take some home with you. Bon Ton specializes in delicious pastries, ranging in price from 30¢ to 40¢. The variety is tantalizing: rich, stick-to-the-roof-of-your-mouth cheesecake-meringue squares, napoleons, dobosh tortes, custard-filled chocolate eclairs, hazelnut rolls, linzer tortes, and more.

Bon Ton is generally crowded and a wait can be expected. Time passes rather quickly as both the pastries and the patrons merit observation.

# The Hungarian Restaurant

4146 N. Lincoln
Phone: 248-1003
Parking: Street
B.Y.O.

Mon.-Fri., 4:00 P.M.—10:00 P.M.
Sat.-Sun., Noon—10:00 P.M.
Closed Wednesday

The Hungarian Restaurant is as straightforward as its name. It's an inviting, cozy little place with a marked eastern European flavor. The walls are covered in flower-patterned paper, bunches of plastic flowers and grapes hang about, as do peasant genre paintings. The Hungarian is practically a one-woman operation. Ms. Melik, its owner and cook, is always busy dishing up goulash and strudel in an open kitchen off to one side of the dining room.

Her portions are generally good sized, and an entree plus salad and bread averages $3.25. A particularly outstanding dish is the Burgundy goulash ($3.25), loaded with mushrooms and served with buttery spaetzle. The Szekely goulash ($3.00), a beef-sauerkraut-sour-cream affair, is also exceptional. If you're an experimenter, the combination plate ($4.00) is a good idea. It includes a sampling of chicken paprikash, stuffed cabbage, beef goulash, either meat loaf or smoked pork, and spaetzle.

The bread is nice and crusty, the salad is adequate, and among the soups, liver dumpling is a standout. If you're up for dessert, give a pass to the strudel and share the palascinta, a Hungarian rolled pancake (80¢). Each serving features two light, jam-filled pancakes that quickly melt in your mouth.

Service is very personable, though it can be erratic at peak hours.

# Gaylord

678 N. Clark
Phone: 664-0100
Parking: Lot, across street
Full bar

Mon.-Thur., 11:00 A.M.—2:00 P.M.; 5:30 P.M.—10:30 P.M.
Fri.-Sat., 11:00 A.M.—2:00 P.M.; 5:30 P.M.—11:00 P.M.
Sun., 5:30 P.M.—10:30 P.M.

The attractive Gaylord serves a wide range of carefully prepared Indian dishes. If in doubt, ask the waiters. They are courteous, knowledgeable, and happy to explain the complexities of the menu.

Most everything is a la carte. Going over our $4.50 budget is easy, as the menu is loaded with delicacies that are too good to miss. One dish we especially recommend is tandoori chicken (½ chicken, $2.75; whole, $5.00). It is marinated, then grilled over charcoal in a special clay oven. The result is one of the tenderest and most full-flavored chickens we've ever eaten. Two other excellent tandoori style dishes are boti kabab (small chunks of skewered lamb, $3.00) and seikh kabab (mixed ground lamb, onions and herbs, $3.00).

Curries are also delicious, particularly the vegetarian alu bengan (eggplant and potato, $2.00) and the subtly-flavored roghan josh (lamb curry, $3.00). There's also a mellow chicken jaipuri (cooked in a yogurt sauce and topped with hard boiled egg slices, $2.75) and shajahni (a stew-like dish of chicken, mushrooms, nuts, and herbs, $3.00).

Rice is the perfect complement to the curries, and one order of rice and peas pullau ($1.00) is plenty for three people. Try a side dish of vegetable samosa (40¢), a light deep-fried mix of vegetables and potatoes, something like a knish. The good breads include bubbly-surfaced, pancake-sized nan (50¢) and the keema nan, filled with minced lamb, which is even better ($1.00).

Desserts are sweet and distinctive. We particularly like ras malai ($1.00), a refreshing spongy-textured pudding fashioned from milk and cheese. The unusual candy-like jalabi, made of ground chick pea flour, is much sweeter and tastes like deep-fried perfume.

Fifteen percent service is automatically added to the bill.

# Maharaja

5002 N. Broadway
Phone: 271-0674
528-3868
Parking: Street
B.Y.O.

Thur.-Fri., 6:00 P.M.—10:00 P.M.
Sat.-Sun., 5:00 P.M.—10:00 P.M.
Closed Monday, Tuesday, Wednesday

Maharaja is a friendly, husband-and-wife-run restaurant specializing in authentic Indian food. It is frequented mainly by young Indian couples, though it's starting to catch on with others. Much of the food is spicy by western standards, so be prepared for adventure.

It's possible to pick and choose items (costing 50¢ to $1.50) from various categories, or to order a complete dinner for $4.25 to $4.50. The dinner includes appetizer, dal (a fiery lentil soup), curry, rice pulau (pilaf), bread, dessert, and beverage. Naresh, the owner, waits on tables and is more than willing to answer any questions that may arise about the menu. He manages to handle explanations, steaming bowls of curry, and tote his tiny daughter along all at the same time.

Meanwhile his wife, Smeeta, is busy preparing unusual dishes in the kitchen. Her specialties include succulent Tandoori chicken ($1.50), Masala kofta (three mild meatballs in a sultry sauce, $1.50), and curried chicken Dopiyaza ($1.50). Watch out for the Baingan Alu-tomato (eggplant curry, $1.60), unless you're prepared to burn. Razor thin, crisp crepes are excellent, particularly the coriander spiced cheese Dosa ($1.50).

You could live here by bread alone. The puris (50¢ for two) is a hollow, blimp-shaped puff. Nan (65¢ for one) is a flatter, buttery grilled bread, and batura (65¢ for two) is light, delicate and puffy. Be sure to also try the "Healthy Drinks" (80¢) There's Lassi, a frothy, semi-sweet iced yogurt concoction, fresh icy mango, or banana drinks, and a sweeter combination of rosewater and milk.

Desserts are also exotic, especially the Burfi (70¢), a fudge-textured cake covered with silver leaf.

Maharaja has a nice, warm feeling about it. There are only five tables, but they're large, so people often share.

# Sabra Kosher Restaurant

2712 W. Pratt
Phone: 764-3563
Parking: Street
No liquor

Daily, Noon—10:00 P.M.
Closed Friday at sundown until Saturday at sundown.

Whether you have a taste for exotic Middle Eastern cooking or more earthy eastern European fare, you'll find either at Sabra. It's an Israeli-kosher restaurant that combines the best of both. Shish kabob and musaka share the menu with brisket and goulash. There's pita bread and soft, fluffy rolls, rice pilaf and potatoes. The restaurant is strictly meat only, meaning no dairy products are permitted either in the cooking or at the table.

However this shouldn't cramp anyone too much. There are several exciting things on the menu. We recommend you start by sharing a combination plate ($2.00) of Middle Eastern appetizers—homos, tehina (sesame spread) and deep fried felafel balls. The plate is attractively served and all three are delicious. It comes with pita bread for dipping. You might also consider the Israeli salad—tomato, cucumber, green pepper, oil, and lemon (95¢) or the eggplant salad ($1.00). Soups are good too, particularly the gusty tomato-based lima bean soup (50¢).

Middle Eastern dinners include shish kabob made from either beef, lamb, or a combination ($4.25), pashtida (a noodle-meat casserole similar to Greek pastitsio, $2.75), and a decent musaka ($2.75). However, we generally prefer their non-Middle Eastern entrees—goulash ($3.25), brisket ($3.25), and baked chicken ($3.25). Goulash is particularly tasty, as it's made of tender brisket chunks simmered in a light green pepper-flavored tomato sauce. Entrees are accompanied by rice pilaf, vegetable (usually canned peas and carrots), and excellent soft rolls.

Desserts we could do without. The baklava (50¢) is too soggy, and the ice cream cake (50¢) made of non-dairy ice cream tastes like it. However the rest of the meal is both filling and tasty, making dessert somewhat superfluous anyway.

# Cas and Lou's

3457 W. Irving Park
Phone: 588-8445
Parking: Street
Full bar

Daily, 11:00 A.M.—10:00 P.M.
Fri.-Sat., 11:00 A.M.—3:00 A.M.
Sun., 1:00 P.M.—10:00 P.M.

Cas and Lou's began about ten years ago as a corner deli. Customers would spot the Aiello family munching something good in the back room and ask for a sample. Instead of continuing to give their dinner away, the Aiellos gradually eliminated selling groceries and took to cooking them. Happily for us, because the food is both good and cheap. They have recently expanded by adding an adjacent dining room which has three levels and is seeped in a rustic country charm. Service is spirited and friendly.

The food is fine here, and the kitchen dishes up several pastas and also a more limited selection of meat entrees. The pastas range from $1.00 for noodles with tomato sauce up to $2.95 for lasagna, the house specialty. All come with garlic bread, in case you need a little extra starch. Meat dinners—meatballs, Italian beef or sausage, pizzaburger—average $2.50 and include salad, potato, and garlic bread.

Linguini with clam sauce is done up well (lots of clams, $2.50) as is the spaghetti with garlic-butter sauce ($1.95). The giant-sized portion of lasagna is cheesy and laced with a gentle tomato sauce. Minestrone is decent but the antipasto is a better bet as a starter. It's an impressive conglomerate of cheese, tomatoes, peppers, prosciutto, salami, bologna, and olive salad.

No matter how much you've eaten, try to save a bit of space for the freshest, most ambrosiac cannoli around (50¢). The crunchy shell, smooth rich ricotta filling, and healthy sprinkling of pistachios and powdered sugar make it irresistible!

Cas and Lou's also prepares a wide variety of sandwiches. They're served on crusty bread, and among the most appealing are prosciutto and provolone (95¢), meat ball (95¢) and fried egg, pepper and mozzarella (95¢).

# *Febo's

2501 S. Western
Phone: 523-0839
Parking: Lot, on Western Avenue
Full bar

Daily, 11:00 A.M.—Midnight
Fri.-Sat., 11:00 A.M.—1:00 A.M.
Closed Sunday
Reservations suggested

The search for an inexpensive Italian restaurant that goes beyond the usual pasta dishes need not take you to Florence or Bologna. There's one right here on Chicago's near southwest side. Febo's prices are slightly higher than our other budget Italian eateries, but dinners include appetizer and soup as well as dessert.

Most meals are priced from $3.50 to $4.50, other than higher priced steak and veal dishes. We suggest you begin your meal with an antipasto plate—it's attractively arranged and each person gets his own. Fresh, chewy Fontana bread goes along nicely. Soup's next, and minestrone (available Wednesday, Friday and Saturday only) is the standout. The salad sports more ingredients than usual and a welcome gathering of herbs.

However, the entrees are what Febo's is all about. The linguine Alfredo ($3.95) with its garlicky butter-cheese sauce is both delicate and potent. Baked green noodles ($3.75), tortellini a la Bolognese ($3.95), and super rich cannelloni ($3.95) are also far from ordinary.

Our favorite dish at Febo's is their chicken Alfredo ($4.50). The juicy sauteed chicken is smothered with mushrooms and served in a lemon-herb seasoned wine sauce along with artichoke hearts and crisp whole new potatoes. The exquisite sister dish, Chicken Vesuvio ($4.50), comes minus the mushrooms and artichokes but with some equally tantalizing long crisp potatoes.

Dessert choices include a disappointing cannoli (it's been frozen), spumoni, and an excellent tortoni crowned with whipped cream.

Febo's is a huge, permanently crowded place that is laid out in a series of small dining rooms. In one of the rooms seating can be had in old, high-back wooden booths that look like they were lifted out of a European train.

# La Fontanella

2414 S. Oakley
Phone: 927-5249
Parking: Street
Full bar

Daily, 11:00 A.M.—Midnight
Sat.-Sun., 4:30 P.M.—Midnight
Closed Monday

La Fontanella is the perfect movie-set neighborhood Italian restaurant. It could easily be in Brooklyn, but luckily it's in Chicago. The feeling is friendly, warm, and storefront cozy. Franca Desideri cooks, her husband, Guido, minds bar and helps attend tables, and daughter, Isabella, is the waitress. Food is made to order, so plan on relaxing. The prices will relax you even further as they are comfortably low.

Their menu is ambitious for such a small operation. Not only are there the usual pastas (ranging from $1.75 to $2.25), but also saltimbocca, veal scallopini with artichokes, and frittata, an Italian omelette. One of our favorite dishes is chicken a la Franca ($4.00), a specialty of the house. Each piece is lightly fried and bursts with a filling of butter, herbs, and parmesan cheese. Pan fried potatoes and artichokes make an unbeatable accompaniment. Saltimbocca ($4.75), a delectable medley of thin sliced veal, prosciutto and mushrooms, is gently seasoned and sauced. Veal scallopini, with either artichokes or mushrooms ($4.50) is delicious as is the chicken cacciatore ($4.50).

La Fontanella also prepares an interesting Sicilian dish called arancini, deep fried balls of rice stuffed with marble-sized meatballs ($2.00). It is served with a rich meat sauce on the side, plus a small antipasto. They do pizza here too, but while it's nice and cheesy, we found the crust a little too soggy.

All meat and chicken entrees, other than arancini, come with either a full-bodied minestrone thick with green noodles and white beans or a rather ordinary salad. You also have your choice of either potatoes or a good mostaccioli cooked al dente. To round out the meal, there's a nice crusty Italian bread, beverage, and dessert. Besides superb cannoli, you usually have a choice which includes spumoni, tortoni, chocolate eclairs and napoleons.

# Gennaro's

1352 W. Taylor
Phone: 243-1035
733-8790
Parking: Street
Full bar

Daily, 5:00 P.M.—9:00 P.M.
Fri.-Sat., 5:00 P.M.—10:00 P.M.
Closed Monday

Gennaro's retains some of the flavor of the speakeasy days. The front door is often locked and you usually have to knock solidly to gain admittance. But once you enter, it's all pretty straight. The TV is on, and most people are thoroughly engaged in scarfing down big platesful of spaghetti. The walls are covered with glossy paneling, fish trophies, and photographs.

The compact menu centers on its homemade pasta and pizza. All of the noodle dishes cost under $2.50. Standouts are the gnocchi (chewy, potato noodles) with tomato sauce ($2.10) and the cheese-filled ravioli ($2.10). A meatball or sausage addition costs 60¢ more. The linguine isn't mixed and rolled in Gennaro's kitchen, but you can have it topped by an unusual anchovy, garlic, and oil sauce ($2.30).

The term "small" pizza ($3.25) is a misnomer. The one we received practically covered the table. It can easily serve four when combined with a pasta dish or two. The crust is thin and crunchy, while the topping is spicy and well-laden with cheese. We found the sausage pizzas to be a bit sparse on the meat, though.

Accompany your starch with a gigantic antipasto ($1.20 per person). They're so enormous that the meats are served on one plate and the vegetables on another.

Desserts are available, including spumoni, tortoni, or homemade cannoli with either a chocolate or vanilla filling. There are several Italian wines to wash it all down.

# *Mategrano's

1321 W. Taylor
Phone: 243-8441
Parking: Rear lot and street
Full bar

Mon.-Fri., 11:00 A.M.—9:30 P.M.
Sat., 4:00 P.M.—10:00 P.M.
Thur. and Sat. buffet, 5:00 P.M.—9:00 P.M.
Closed Sunday

If you've never attended an Italian wedding feast, Mategrano's offers a good substitute. On Thursday and Saturday nights they present an all-you-can-eat buffet for $3.75 that will challenge the most gargantuan appetite. The buffet is made up of eighteen or so Italian specialties, many of them unusual.

A typical spread includes various pastas, perhaps a lasagna, mostaccioli and macaroni pie. There's herb-seasoned baked chicken, homemade Italian sausage, and a savory beef and green bean stew. The thick, meaty eggplant parmigiana is delicious and so are the ricotta cheese puffs.

Vegetables aren't neglected. There are batter-fried zucchini strips, cold marinated zucchini slices, an escarole and white bean combination, green bean salad, and marinated whole sweet peppers. Don't skip the pizza bread, but go light on the limp and soggy tossed salad.

Each trip to the buffet will bring a new surprise, so use restraint and keep an eye on the waitresses bearing platters from the kitchen. Better things may be yet to come! There are also small pitchers of light, homemade red wine, but they're priced a little high at $2.50.

Be sure to call in for reservations on buffet nights because Mategrano's is packed with people—all eating like there's no tomorrow. And it's a good place to be just in case there isn't.

On non-buffet nights the menu includes a wide variety of interesting pasta dishes all priced under $3.00.

# Toscano's

2439 S. Oakley
Phone: 847-8829
Parking: Street
Full bar

Daily, 11:00 A.M.—Midnight
Fri., 11:00 A.M.—1:00 A.M.
Sat., 11:00 A.M.—2:00 A.M.
Sun., Noon—10:00 P.M.
Closed Monday

Tucked away on a southwest side residential street is Toscano's, an unpretentious, neighborhood kind of place. It's crowded, but not too crowded, and very efficiently and smoothly run. It's best to come here with a ravenous appetite.

Complete dinners, which are served from 5:00 to 10:00 P.M., consist of a chewy Italian bread from nearby Fontana's bakery, an above-average minestrone, fresh salad, entree, beverage, and dessert. The menu is loaded with pastas, and includes a choice of six tomato-based sauces, the more interesting being the Italian sausage, chicken liver, or the house specialty, chicken liver and mushroom. The lasagna ($3.55), as the menu suggests, is "truly a treat." The broad noodles are prepared al dente, layered between a subtle meat sauce, and topped by a thick, sizzling layer of melted mozzarella.

There is also a selection of chicken and veal dishes, most priced higher than our $4.50 budget. Try the chicken, Toscano-style ($3.50). Resembling cacciatiore, the meat is cooked tender in a flavorful wine-spiked tomato-mushroom sauce. It's very tasty, though the sauce could have more mushrooms.

Portions are large at Toscano's, but try to save room for dessert. Rather than spumoni or tortoni, spend 20¢ extra for some excellent cannoli. The shell is fresh and crunchy and the ricotta filling is scrumptiously rich.

# Ichiban

3155 N. Broadway
Phone: 935-3636
Parking: Difficult
Full bar

Mon.-Thur., 5:00 P.M.—11:00 P.M.
Fri., 5:00 P.M.—Midnight
Sat., Noon—Midnight
Sun., Noon—10:00 P.M.

Ichiban is the most attractive budget-priced Japanese restaurant in town. It looks like a far-Eastern Crate and Barrel—clean design, lots of wood, colorful pillows, and globular rice paper lamp shades. It makes for a serene, comfortable setting where, happily, the food is given as much attention as the decor. Cooking is done in an efficient and spotless open kitchen where each step of the process can be observed, particularly if you happen to sit at the bar.

The concise menu concentrates on tempura and teriyaki, with the tempura getting a nod. A tempura dinner ($3.10) includes shrimp, bermuda onion slice, green pepper, and a pile of slivered sweet potatoes. All are coated with the lightest of batters, and the sweet potatoes, in particular, are outstanding. For something slightly different, give the kakiage tempura patties ($2.50) a try. They're a feathery concoction of deep fried vegetables and shrimp. Ichiban also does a nice thing by making individual tempura vegetables or shrimp available as side dishes (50¢ to 75¢).

Of the three teriyakis—chicken ($2.75), pork ($2.80), or beef ($2.90)—we prefer the chicken. It has a nice charcoal flavor, and the portion is large. However, the teriyaki sauce, rather than being a subtle marinade, is more like a thick sweet and sour syrup. It's tasty, but not for traditionalists.

Other entrees are a somewhat ordinary sweet and sour pork ($2.90), pepper beef and tomato ($2.90), and ramein, a large potful of noodle-vegetable soup that makes a fine budget meal ($1.50). All main dishes, with the exception of the ramein, include fried rice, a zippy marinated slaw, and tea. If you wish something stronger to sip, there's a nice selection of Japanese wine and beer.

Another, newer Ichiban is located at 1660 N. La Salle (phone: 649-1000). Their menu is more expansive, and there are special teppan tables where cooking is done before you.

# Miyako

3242 N. Clark
Phone: 549-1085
Parking: Street
B.Y.O.

Daily, Noon—10:00 P.M.
Closed Sunday

Miyako is probably Chicago's cheapest Japanese restaurant. All entrees cost under $3.00, and several are below $2.00. It's setting is nothing to write home about, but it's a clean place and the food is both delicious and authentic.

There is a wide selection of entrees ranging from ever-popular tempura and teriyaki to more rare kayaku (eel) udon ($1.85) and abalone sashimi ($2.60). All meals include a clear but filling broth, a small dish of pickled vegetables, and a pot of mild brewed tea. Rice is 15¢ extra per person. Appetizers of pickled gomaye (spinach, 60¢) and sunomono (cucumber, 60¢) are excellent.

The sukiyaki at $2.95 is the most expensive item on the menu, but it is served in a portion big enough for two. Tender thin-sliced beef, nappa (cabbage), fresh mushrooms, scallions, and thin transparent saifun noodles share a slightly sweet broth. The sukiyaki is well-made and flavorful, as are the udon dishes. These are basically large bowls of soup containing long, somewhat thick noodles to which a variety of ingredients may be added. Try the tempura udon ($2.10) which features batter-fried shrimp, green beans, and squash or nabeyaki udon ($1.85), a blend of chicken, egg, and vegetables. The donburi or rice-based dishes are not only tasty, but put your skill with chopsticks to the test. (Silverware is served only upon request.)

The expertly-prepared tempura ($2.60) has a crisp, light batter. The three large butterfly shrimp are firm and fresh-tasting and come with equally delicate batter-fried sweet potato, eggplant, and green beans. Beef teriyaki ($2.30) is the lowest-priced around, the portion is generous, and the meat well-marinated and tender.

As characteristic of most Japanese restaurants, service at Miyako's is both unobtrusive and efficient. Portions are large, and it's easy for two people to enjoy a satisfying dinner for under $6.00.

# Naniwa

923 W. Belmont
Phone: 348-9027
Parking: Street
B.Y.O.

Daily, 4:00 P.M.—10:00 P.M.
Sat.-Sun., Noon—10:00 P.M.
Closed Wednesday

Naniwa's setting is plain storefront, and service can occasionally be disinterested. However, it features some fine Japanese cooking at very pleasing prices. Located next door to Ann Sather's, Naniwa's offers an altogether different atmosphere. The room is somewhat somber and bare of decoration, but a taste of beef teriyaki or shrimp tempura will immediately dissolve any temporary blahs.

The menu is lengthy and features several Japanese specialties, most of which are $2.50 or under. All entrees include a small dish of pickled vegetables, a large covered bowl of rice, and a pot of brewed tea. There are a variety of udon (noodle dishes), nabe (soups), and donburi (meat, vegetables, and rice), as well as the more usual but well-prepared teriyaki and tempura.

Try oyako donburi ($1.75), bits of chicken, scrambled egg, bamboo shoots, and onions seasoned with a saki-sugar-soy sauce mixture and served on a bed of rice. The portion is large, and the combination of flavors is delicious. Pork or beef nabe ($2.25) is a healthful, flavorsome soup featuring thin noodles, meat, soy curd, and assorted vegetables, including fresh mushrooms. It is served in a black iron pot and acts as a restorative, especially on an icy winter day. There is also a more unusual ika (squid) nabe ($2.25). They prepare beef teriyaki ($2.50) with finesse here. Thinly sliced meat is served in a light, not too sweet teriyaki sauce that tastes marvelous with the rice. Tempura and sashimi (marinated raw fish) are slightly more expensive at $3.00, but both are quite good.

# Tenkatsu

3365 N. Clark
Phone: 549-8697
Parking: Street
B.Y.O.

Daily, 5:00 P.M.—10:00 P.M.
Closed Tuesday

A simpler and more unpretentious place than Tenkatsu would be hard to find. Recent remodeling has spruced it up a bit, though the food has never needed any redoing. Most dishes cost well under $4.00 and portions are generous. All meals include a small dish of spicy pickled cabbage, a soup containing soybean curd and scallions, and tea. Teriyaki and tempura are served with rice.

One of our favorites is beef yasai ($3.00), an impressive mound of thin tender beef slices, fresh bean sprouts, bamboo shoots, fried onions, scallions, and transparent noodles in a semisweet soy broth. It's a cozy blend of flavors and textures, and is quite delicious. The udon (noodle soup, $2.15) has a slightly smoky taste, is very filling, and makes a terrific bargain meal, especially with a tempura addition (called "tempura udon").

Another great dish is the donburi ($2.50). It is prepared several ways, two of the best being oyako (chicken and egg) and niku (beef and egg). These ingredients plus fresh mushrooms, bamboo shoots, fried onions, scallions, and transparent noodles are piled atop a bed of rice. This dish always gets better and better while you eat it, as the rice keeps soaking in more of the juice. Beef teriyaki ($3.00) and shrimp tempura ($3.25) are both reliable and well-prepared.

# Ashkenaz

1432 W. Morse
Phone: 465-5392
Parking: Street
No liquor

Daily, 10:30 A.M.—10:30 P.M.
Sat.-Sun., 6:00 A.M.—10:30 P.M.

If you'd like to hear about Judy's sweet sixteen party, Nathan's new apartment, or Harriet's no-good son-in-law, go to Ashkenaz. If you're more interested in some fine cabbage soup, grilled reubens, or sweet-and-sour meatballs, this is still your place. Complete dinners include appetizer (a choice from among four herring dishes, chopped liver, gefiltefish) or soup, a basket of fresh rolls, salad or slaw, meat, vegetable, potato, beverage and dessert.

Soups are generally good and filling. The cabbage soup is a perfect blend of sweet and sour, and the blenderized beet borscht contains about a pint of sour cream. Chicken soup is just average, but either the two fluffy matzoh balls or kreplach more than compensate for the pallid broth. Mushroom-barley, with a tomato base, is disappointing.

As a main course, the sweet-and-sour meat dishes are always excellent, particularly the juicy, full-bodied sweet-and-sour cabbage meat ($4.10). The roast or boiled brisket ($4.20) are also good as are the gefilte fish ($3.30) and chicken in the pot (a one dish meal containing chicken, matzoh ball, kreplach, noodles, and vegetables in broth, $3.95).

Vegetables and potatoes are easily forgotten, but the cole slaw is creamy, the rolls are fresh and the rye bread, chewy. For dessert it's hard to object to pineapple cheesecake or chocolate layer cake. Ashkenaz also makes a great hot fudge sundae.

For a lighter meal, try the lox and cream cheese plate ($3.25), grilled reuben ($2.10), or, heaven forbid, a Joey Bishop (a triple decker corned beef and swiss cheese combo, $1.90). There's pastrami ($1.35), pickled tongue ($1.35) and even a better-than-average hamburger ($1.50 or $2.10). Blintzes ($1.90) are too heavy, and the potato pancakes ($1.80) aren't bad until they hit you at the second to last bite.

# *The Bagel

4806 N. Kedzie — Daily, 5:00 A.M.—9:00 P.M.
Phone: 463-7141
Parking: Street
No liquor

You don't have to be Jewish to enjoy The Bagel. It's for anyone with an urge to feast on healthy portions of good, Jewish "soul food", served up with a bit of mothering. The Bagel is a simple store front located in the old Jewish neighborhood around Lawrence and Kedzie. There's a warm familiarity in the place, and lots of kibbitzing between the crowd and the waitresses.

However, the main business of the establishment is its food, and there's plenty of it. Dinners run between $3.25 and $3.75 and include appetizer or soup, apple sauce, cole slaw or salad, meat, potato, vegetables, dessert, and beverage.

As soon as you sit down, the waitress places a plate of crisp, kosher dills on your table. This is soon followed by a basket filled with pumpernickel bread and thick slices of Challe (egg bread), which keeps getting refilled.

There are some beautiful starters: fresh pickled herring, moist chopped liver, matzoh ball soup on Friday, kreplach on Wednesday, and, frequently, mushroom-barley.

Main courses vary. There might be a Polish-style white fish stuffed with gefilte fish ($3.50) or a cold, pickled sweet and sour white fish ($3.50). Rich, juicy baked veal breast ($3.75) is served in a football-sized portion while baked brisket ($3.75) is somewhat smaller. Along with the meat you may luck upon a crisp potato or noodle kugel (pudding). Vegetables are not the high point of Jewish cooking, and the canned peas and carrots at The Bagel are no exception, though your waitress will keep urging you to try some. If you still can make it, there's a nice custard-like rice pudding for dessert.

Nothing is cooked fancy at The Bagel. It's just good stick-to-your-ribs-forever fare.

For Sunday breakfast, fried herring and great, enormous scrambled omelettes are served. Try the Spanish or the Denver.

# Frances'

2453 N. Clark
Phone: 525-9675
Parking: Street (difficult)
No liquor

Tue.-Sun., 6:00 A.M.—Midnight
Closed Monday

Where would Clark Street be without Frances' to feed its broke but hungry citizens? The place has a passionate following for good reason. There is always something warm and nourishing to be had at prices that rival those of the Bohemian restaurants on the southwest side. An onion-smothered hamburger the size of a 16″ softball, plus three side dishes will cost you $1.65. A duck dinner is only $2.75. And there's a wide variety in between: beef stew ($2.55), meat loaf ($1.95), veal breast ($2.75), turkey leg ($2.55), roast chicken ($2.10), and more.

The side dishes vary in type and appeal. Among the best are the kishke and the noodles. The cole slaw has a nice flavor, though it tends to be soupy, and most of the vegetables are best forgotten unless you're partial to food straight from the can. There's always a good supply of excellent, chewy rye bread.

Food is displayed steam table fashion. You make your selection, choose a seat, and wait for the waitress to bring the order. It all looks surprisingly more appealing on your plate, and most meals not only fill you up but are downright tasty.

Frances' makes no attempt at decoration, other than a few signs touting grilled reubens or fried matzoh. If you're a strict adherent of the "cleanliness is next to godliness" maxim, don't look too hard. The place gets a little raunchy as the evening winds down. But if you're after an inexpensive hot meal, try Frances'.

# Seoul House

5346 N. Clark
Phone: 728-6756
Parking: Street
B.Y.O.

Daily, 11:00 A.M.—11:00 P.M.
Closed Tuesday

For a different kind of Seoul food, this is the place. A popular restaurant with local Koreans, everything here is fresh, flavorful, and carefully cooked to order. Korean food, while related to other Oriental cuisines, has its own distinct identity characterized by unique combinations of ingredients and slightly unusual, heartier sauces.

All meals come with individual, covered silver bowls of hot steamed rice, pickled vegetables (quite spicy), and tea. Chopsticks, rather than silverware, are placed at each setting. A good opportunity to put them to work is with an appetizer of fried mahndoo (45¢ for 2 pieces), puffy meat-filled turnovers that are a cross between won ton and egg roll.

A charcoaled meat dish is worth ordering for its aroma alone. You have your choice from among fire meat—thin sliced grilled beef that is not a mouth-burner as its name might imply ($3.15), gahlbee, charcoaled short ribs ($2.95), and sanjuk, a blend of charcoaled sirloin cubes, mushrooms, green peppers, tomatoes, and scallions ($3.25). In each dish, the meat is given a lengthy marinating before actual grilling.

Some other dishes that have special appeal are chop chae, a sauteed mixture of beef, mushrooms, shredded carrots, scallions, and glossy noodles ($2.65), tahng suyuck, a close relative of sweet and sour pork but with a more pungent vinegar sauce ($2.85), and dalhk bokem, plump juicy chunks of chicken stir-fried with green peppers, onions, carrots, and fungus in a sweet salty sauce ($2.75). Perhaps our favorite dish, however, is the beef, shrimp, and abalone with fresh, crisp vegetables ($3.65). It's a feast of textures and tastes. Last time we tried it, the abalone were among the best we've ever eaten and had just the right slightly chewy (but not rubbery) texture.

# Healthy Food Restaurant

3236 S. Halsted
Phone: 326-2724
Parking: Street
No liquor

Daily, 7:00 A.M.—8:00 P.M.
Sun., 8:00 A.M.—8:00 P.M.

Located in Mayor Daley's Bridgeport community, this isn't an organic food spot as its name might imply. Rather, it's a simple neighborhood restaurant featuring healthy portions of good, Lithuanian home-cooking. The interior is somewhat dark and gloomy, looking a bit like a lost relative of the old Marquis Lunches. The menu will pep you up considerably, as practically all meals, including dessert, cost between $1.85 and $2.50. A large bowl of soup is 25¢ extra.

The breads are a tour through the rye: black rye, light rye, and a marvelous spongy-textured buttermilk rye. Every day there are two robust soups: perhaps a sauerkraut, chicken noodle, vegetable, barley, or hot beet. In the summer, don't miss the fantastic cold beet borscht garnished with sour cream and fresh dill.

Dinner specials vary each day, and feature such basics as short ribs ($2.50), chicken livers ($2.30), thin sliced, tender beef liver with either onions or bacon ($2.30), pork chops ($3.25), and a strangely spiced meat loaf ($1.85). Vegetables, potatoes, and salad are included. Be sure to request the pan-fried potatoes, as they're golden crisp on the outside and soft and tender inside. Also, we suggest asking them to go easy on the gravy.

If you're in the mood for something lighter, Healthy Food makes some great blynas: rich, eggy pancakes folded envelope-style around cheese, blueberry, or apple filling. They're dusted with powdered sugar, served with sour cream, and are unbelievably good.

Though we've never spotted the mayor downing blynas, lots of folks from his neighborhood dine at Healthy Food.

# Neringa

2632 W. 71st
Phone: 776-1018
Parking: Street
No liquor

Daily, 8:00 A.M.—8:00 P.M.
Closed Wednesday

Located at the corner of an orderly row of houses in insular Marquette Park, the Neringa is another fine Lithuanian restaurant. Superficially the restaurant looks no different from any other corner coffee shop in the city, though one look at the menu will dispel any desire to order a BLT on toast. The Neringa boasts an expansive yet inexpensive list of Lithuanian specialties. Complete meals, including salad and a light dessert, are priced between $1.90 and $2.35.

There's a fine selection of breads: raisin, a chewy anise-flavored rye, and a regular rye. Soups are 50¢ to 60¢ extra, but the cold beet borscht is worth it. It's loaded with chopped cucumbers, hard boiled egg, chives, and sour cream as well as beets. And it comes with a boiled potato served on the side. The sauerkraut soup is reliable, but we recommend skipping the beef and barley.

Choosing a main course can be traumatic, for there are just too many tempters. Meat blintzes ($2.30), stuffed cabbage ($2.00), cepelinai (meat-filled potato dumplings, $1.95), mushroom dumplings ($1.95), thuringer with kraut ($2.00), roast duck ($2.50), and more. The meat blintzes ($2.20) are exceptionally tasty, but the real highlight are the rolled pancakes filled with a perfect cranberry sauce ($2.10) that is neither too sweet nor too tart. Top them with sour cream, and you're in heaven.

The Neringa is big, clean, and usually bustling. Most of your fellow diners are from the neighborhood, and all of them seem to know a good bargain when they see one.

# Tulpe (Tulip)

2447 W. 69th
Phone: 925-1123
Parking: Street
No liquor

Daily, 7:00 A.M.—8:00 P.M.
Sun., 7:00 A.M.—7:00 P.M.

Walking into the Tulpe, you get a flash of how a stranger must have felt upon entering a bar in Tombstone. The cooks stare, the waitresses stare, and customers stare because this is essentially a tight, neighborhood place that sees few outsiders. It's also very tiny, so if the three tables and minute counter are filled, you have to stand inside the doorway looking about as inconspicuous as Alice Cooper at a DAR convention. However, once you settle in, no one is really unsocial, and the food and prices are friendly as can be.

Complete meals, which include soup, salad, dessert, and beverage, run between $1.90 and $2.80. It's easy to devour the basketful of Latvian sour rye. But move easily. Next there's a big bowl of sauerkraut soup (or something equally delicate!) served with a boiled potato on the side. Main dishes vary, and some worth sampling are the kotletai patties (a cross between meatballs and meatloaf), roast pork with sauerkraut, liver and onions, beef stew, and fabulous Lithuanian pancakes filled with cranberry, cheese, or apple.

Dessert is usually something unexciting, like a dish of canned fruit. However, it's about all you can eat anyway.

Just as we were about to leave, a young waitress enthusiastically urged us to return, dispelling any lingering doubts that outsiders are not wanted at the Tulpe.

# La Choza

7630 N. Paulina
Phone: 465-9401
Parking: Street
B.Y.O.

Tue.-Fri., Noon—11:30 P.M.
Sat., Noon—Midnight
Sun., Noon—10:30 P.M.
Closed Monday

Take a small room, load it with a carnival of decorations, wall-to-wall tables and booths, and you wonder how people are going to fit in. But they do, and miraculously everything runs quite comfortably and smoothly at this always popular, northside Mexican restaurant. The feeling comes out cozy rather than cramped, especially if you don't mind sharing the boarding house table that bisects the restaurant.

By all means start your meal with their cheesy kamoosh (deep-fried tortillas with melted cheese) ($1.10 for 2 people; $1.60 for 4), easily one of the most luscious dishes around. It takes restraint not to grab all the pieces yourself. The rich, mild, guacamole ($1.35) is good too.

Besides the standard taco-tostada circuit, La Choza prepares steak eleven different ways. You can have it with ranchero (spicy tomato) sauce ($3.95), sauteed with green peppers, tomatoes, and onions ($3.95), or stuffed into a flour tortilla along with avocado sauce and a covering of piquant Indian sauce ("burrochoza", $3.95). We particularly like Steak Oaxaca ($3.95), in which strips of sirloin steak are topped by a harmonious blend of finely chopped onions, tomatoes, parsley, and melted white Mexican cheese. The whole thing is piled on a tortilla and tastes scrumptious. If you'd like it fiery, request an addition of hot peppers.

The Choza combination plate ($2.95) is a good one and includes a cheese enchilada, beef taco, and mild chile relleno. Avocado tostadas ($2.50) are delicious as are the flautas, three soft tortillas filled with chicken, beef, or sausage and enveloped in an avocado and sour cream topping ($2.50). All meals include rice and beans and begin with crisp tortillas and hot sauce.

We recommend closing your meal with mango pudding (65¢). It's creamy, very fruity-tasting, and very sweet.

# Mexican Food

948 W. Webster
Phone: 525-9793
Parking: Street
B.Y.O.

Daily, Noon—10:00 P.M.
Closed Tuesday

One of our favorite Mexican restaurants is tucked behind a hanging sign that simply states, "Mexican Food". Although long popular with young neighborhood residents, it's the kind of place you could walk by five times a day without noticing. However, don't let its nondescript appearance keep you from entering and sampling some delicious, fairly inexpensive Mexican food.

Their tostadas ($1.80) are artfully made—a perfect balance of crisp tortilla, beans, meat, lettuce, and cheese. It's possible to sample three different kinds from among chicken, ground beef, chorizo, and avocado. The latter are particularly scrumptious. Flautas ($2.65) are another attraction. They're fat with chicken and doused with a smooth avocado-sour cream sauce. The delicately spiced Mexican beef stew ($3.00) is quite good—tender chunks of meat simmered in a subtle tomato-inspired sauce. The stew comes with a salad, beans, rice, and a basket of warm tortillas. The combination plate ($2.75) is the usual offering of taco, tostada, enchilada, rice, and beans. The fresh-tasting beans are exceptionally well made, and the rice is tasty. For the more adventurous, breaded tongue and menudo (tripe) are on the menu.

The swiftness of the service depends upon the size of the crowd. If there are more than three or four tables filled, expect a wait. The atmosphere is friendly and similar to a Mexican home where nothing is rushed.

# *Mi Casa, Su Casa

2525 N. Southport
Phone: 525-5028
Parking: Street or lot, 1 block south
Full bar

Daily, 11:00 A.M.—2:00 P.M.; 5:00 P.M.—11:00 P.M.
Fri.-Sat., 5:00 P.M.—2:00 A.M.
Sun., 5:00 P.M.—11:00 P.M.

Mi Casa, Su Casa serves beautifully prepared Mexican food. While the left side of the menu contains more expensive beef dishes, the right side features several moderately priced Mexican specialties. Portions are generous, and all entrees come with rice and some very good refried beans. Food is cooked to order here, and it is generally quite mild.

To start off a meal, try the camuch ($1.50 for ten pieces) —it's the best we've ever tasted. The crisp tortilla chips are covered with beans and mild tomato sauce, and are dripping with melted cheese. A dollop of guacamole is popped on top, and the whole thing tastes fantastic.

Particularly good here are the sumptuous enchiladas. The enchiladas Indias ($2.50) are crisper-than-usual tortillas filled with ground beef and topped with green sauce and gooey melted cheese. Enchiladas suizas ($2.75) are indecently caloric. They're stuffed with chicken and bathed in tomato sauce, melted cheese, and sour cream. Enchiladas with homemade chorizo (sausage) are also a possibility ($3.25).

Another treat here are the sopes ($2.50). Homemade tortillas are hand-patted into rowboat shape and topped with ground beef, beans, tomato, shredded lettuce, and grated cheese. They are delicious and offer a change from the usual tacos and tostadas.

The atmosphere at Mi Casa, Su Casa is a somewhat incongruous combination of neighborhood bar (complete with turned-on TV) and a fancier-than-usual Mexican restaurant. The tables are layered with red and white checked and solid red linen tablecloths. Lighting is subdued and a cozy, almost romantic feeling prevails.

# El Nuevo Leon

1515 W. 18th
Phone: 421-1517
Parking: Street
No liquor

Daily, 8:00 A.M.—3:00 A.M.
Fri.-Sat., 8:00 A.M.—6:00 A.M.

El Nuevo Leon is a bustling neighborhood restaurant filled with Mexican-American families and young couples. It seems to be the most popular place on 18th Street. There are several reasons for its success. The food is good, the prices moderate, and the service is some of the fastest this side of McDonald's.

The menu contains most standard items, plus a few not so standard, like tacos with brains, and chilaquiles (a fried tortilla, scrambled egg, and tomato mixture, $1.90). Tacos ($1.50) aren't extraordinary, but the tacos barbacoa with steamed, shredded beef are chewy and good. The combination plate ($2.40)—taco, tostada, enchilada, and tamale—offers a diverse sampling at a low price. The tamale, with its shredded beef filling, is quite tasty, and the chicken-filled enchilada is bathed in mild, melted cheese. Rice and beans aren't included, so if you can't do without, it will cost you 50¢ more. The ground beef and potato filled chile relleno ($2.50) is the real thing—very hot and spicy. It is available weekends only.

The thick and stew-like beef soup contains good-sized chunks of beef and often a fresh piece of corn on the cob ($1.65). Guacamole ($1.30 for a small order) is priced a bit high for its Lilliputian size.

The decor at El Nuevo Leon is standard Mexican restaurant: velvet paintings on paneled walls, salmon-colored vinyl booths, and a big day-glo jukebox. It's a friendly, lively place, and if you're ever hit by those "wish I were in Mexico blues," it offers a good substitute.

# El Tipico

1836 W. Foster
Phone: 878-0839
Parking: Lot in rear
Full bar

Tue.-Sun., 11:30 A.M.—2:00 A.M.
Closed Monday

From the outside, El Tipico looks more expensive than it is. Though it isn't as cheap as our other Mexican restaurants, it offers by far the most handsome setting, with its stuccoed white walls, beamed, bi-level dining area, and comfortable wood and leather basket chairs. While the menu includes several higher-priced beef entrees, there are many dishes for under $3.25.

Enchiladas are a specialty here, with five different varieties being offered. The best bet is the Tri-Color Combination ($3.25)—one filled with chicken and topped with green sauce, another with beef covered in melted white cheese, and the third filled with yellow cheese and topped with tomato sauce. The dish also includes beans and too-mushy rice.

Tacos ($2.50) are moist, and offer a choice of ground beef, avocado, chicken, or pork filling. In addition to some standard combination plates, there are several chicken dinners, including one with a tomato based ranchero sauce and another with an excellent green sauce.

El Tipico also features an interesting sampling of appetizers. Besides the always reliable nachos (yet another name for crisp tortillas with melted cheese, $1.20) and guacamole, there are quesadillas (melted cheese-filled soft tortillas, 50¢) and rolled burritos (50¢) filled with mildly spiced sausage. Both taste great, though they're slightly greasy.

Everything is cooked to order here, so it's best to enjoy the wait by downing the bowlful of hot, crispy tortilla chips, along with some Mexican beer.

# Mediterranean House

3910 Dempster, Skokie
Phone: 679-7222
Parking: Lot
B.Y.O.

Daily, 11:00 A.M.—11:00 P.M.
Fri.-Sat., 11:00 A.M.—12:30 A.M.
Closed Monday

Located in Skokie on Dempster's franchise row and looking much like a franchise operation itself, Mediterranean House will fool you. Within its glossy setting is served some far from ordinary, authentic Middle Eastern food. Although Mediterranean House is a serve-yourself place, most of the food is freshly prepared, and prices are low enough so that you can sample several of the excellent exotic entrees and side dishes.

Bc surc to try thc falafil sandwich (90¢), as All-Middle Eastern as the hotdog is All-American. Ground chick peas and spices are shaped into balls, crisply deep fried and placed into a pocket of pita bread along with lettuce, tomatoes, and a tahini (sesame) based dressing. The whole thing tastes great, is far healthier than a hotdog and could easily become a habit. Kibbi (65¢), a deep-fried mixture of cracked wheat stuffed with juicy ground beef, onions, and pine nuts, is delicious too. Shawirma is similar to Greek gyros, and is served with rice pilaf and pita for $2.25 or as a sandwich for $1.25.

The most expensive item on the menu is the combination plate ($3.25), containing shish kabab, shawirma, kifta kabab (spicy, fresh-tasting meatballs), pilaf, lettuce, tomato, and pita. You can make several mix and match sandwiches from this variety.

There are two extraordinary dips: hommos (50¢), a delicious blend of ground chick peas, tahini sauce, onion, and oil, and baba ghanooj (75¢), a mixture of chopped eggplant, tahini, lemon juice, parsley, and garlic. Both go beautifully with pita.

Desserts are seductively displayed. It's best just to look and point. You can always be safe with baklava (50¢), but the katayef (50¢), a pancake stuffed with walnuts and sugar syrup or Harisa (50¢), a semolina-based cake imbedded with pistachios, walnuts, and pine nuts and soaked in a sugar syrup, are both unusual and interesting. Accompany dessert with sweet, grainy Turkish coffee (35¢).

# Middle East Restaurant

5444 S. Damen Daily, Noon—Midnight
Phone: 778-9222
Parking: Lot and street
B.Y.O.

Adjoining a smoke-filled Arab men's social club is the quiet and subdued Middle East Restaurant. Because it's not on most people's regular route, the Middle East remains largely unknown to non-Arabs. Although the cooking is authentic, the rustic, glazed, knotty pine walls give the place the feeling of a north woods hunting lodge, so you may want to play the jukebox or peek into the clubroom next door for a bit of atmosphere.

The Middle East's cook is talented, and it seems as though everything he prepares is both unusual and delicious. The menu lists standard entrees plus several rotating daily specials. However, don't be surprised if your waiter recites a list of specials which in no way coincides with those printed on the menu.

One thing you can always count on is a superb bargain-priced shish kebab ($2.50) and various lamb or beef and vegetable combinations. For instance, there might be a cauliflower, meat, and yogurt trio ($2.50), zucchini and lamb ($2.50), stuffed cabbage ($2.50), and Kefta—ground lamb balls served with either tomato or tahini (sesame) sauce ($2.25). One evening we sampled a marvelous vegetable stew, thick with chunks of tender beef, potatoes, green beans, and cauliflower ($2.00). The food here is most similar to Greek, but we find it to be more subtly seasoned, less oily, and having fewer overcooked vegetables.

Rice pilaf costs extra with the stew-like dishes (50¢-75¢). The salads are extra too, but they're definitely worth it. There are two sizes and prices (75¢ and $1.25), with the smaller being just right for two people. Especially tasty is the Arabian salad, a lively combination of finely chopped tomato, lettuce, cucumber, and parsley, tossed with tahini sauce.

For dessert, the thick, moderately sweet Arabian custard (50¢) is good, especially if you're a tapioca fan. Otherwise they sometimes have kenafa (50¢), syrupy shredded wheat filled with sweet cheese. Accompany either with rich thick coffee (25¢).

# Mabuhay

4622 N. Clark
Phone: 275-3688
Parking: Street
Full bar

Daily, 11:00 A.M.—11:00 P.M.

Mabuhay provides a good, inexpensive place to experiment with Philippine food. Although more than half the menu is filled with Chinese dishes, don't chicken out—try the Philippine ones. Portions are not huge, but the food is cheap so it's best to come here in a group and sample a variety of dishes. Three dishes are about right for two people. Rice is included. The rule here, unless you like to live dangerously, is to let the waitress be your guide. They're very friendly and happy to offer suggestions.

The cuisine is different from any we've ever tasted, although there are definite Chinese overtones. Some interesting and distinctive specialties are pork inihaw (thin sliced, barbequed pork and scallions, $2.95), pork or chicken adobo (chunks of meat, marinated and cooked in vinegar and spices, $2.95), and pansit canton gisado (spaghetti-like noodles sauteed with mushrooms, shrimp, and bits of pork, $2.50). Particularly good is the chicken sotanjon, a glazed mixture of thin, transparent sai foon noodles, diced chicken, celery, scallions, and mushrooms ($3.15). There is also a somewhat strange but interesting vegetable dish, pinacbet—okra, eggplant, and tomato cooked in a fish sauce ($2.95).

More familiar are the appetizers, deep fried shrimp ($1.60), and a delicious crisp eggroll that is unmistakably flavored with peanut butter ($1.25).

For purists, there's kari kari, composed of oxtail, tripe, greenbeans, and peanut butter ($2.65) and four bitter melon dishes—pork ($2.55), chicken ($3.15), shrimp ($3.35), and beef ($2.95)—which call for adventurous tastebuds, two years in the Philippines, or both.

# *Michelle

2568 N. Milwaukee — Daily, 9:00 A.M.—9:00 P.M.
Phone: 384-7882
Parking: Street

Our favorite Polish restaurant is a largely unknown and very authentic place simply called Michelle. It's a plain, almost institutional-looking restaurant, but the warm, pleasant atmosphere makes you feel at home. All the Polish specialties are cooked here—pierogi, nalésniki, bigos, golabki, and kolacky—at prices that would please a Scrooge. Complete dinners, including soup and dessert, cost under $3.50.

It is obvious from the first spoonful that the soups don't come from a can. We especially like their thick barley soup, sprinkled with fresh dill. However, unless you're a czarina (duck blood soup) aficionado, give a pass to Michelle's version. It's unabashedly strong and definitely calls for an acquired taste.

Among the entrees, we recommend the golabki (stuffed cabbage, $2.45), Vienna schnitzel topped with a fried egg ($3.40), a marvelous oxtail stew ($2.65), and the thin honey-colored pancakes called nalésniki ($2.45). They're filled with a slightly tart cheese that is almost custard-like in consistency and accompanied by a dish of sour cream, which helps to make a good thing even better. The real tour de force, however, is bigos ($2.55), a smoky-flavored casserole of sauerkraut, pork, and sliced Polish sausage. It has the heady, well-integrated flavor of a dish that has to have been cooked for hours, perhaps even days.

Side dishes—cole slaw, creamy cucumber salad, potato salad, or the humble boiled potato—are all tasty. Desserts too are homemade, delicious, and not to be missed. We think Michelle's kolacky is the best in town, especially if you get one fresh from the oven (at lunch you have a better chance). The dough is thin, almost strudel-like, and fillings range from plum to poppyseed. They also make a rich, moist lemon cake and thick, cinnamon-sprinkled rice pudding.

# Warsaw Restaurant

820 N. Ashland Avenue
Phone: 666-3052
Parking: Street
Full bar (upstairs)

Daily, 11:00 A.M.—Midnight
Fri., 11:00 A.M.—2:00 A.M.

The Warsaw is a tidy neighborhood place with a primarily Polish-speaking clientele. The emphasis here is on simple, well prepared food served in liberal portions.

The menu features a long lineup of complete dinners, averaging around $3.00, including such Polish specialties as bigos, nalésniki, and pierogi. Try any of them and you'll be satisfied. Bigos ($2.10), or hunter's stew, is a hefty combination of sausage and sauerkraut. The pierogi ($2.60) are sauteed in butter rather than boiled and are filled with your choice of either meat, cabbage, cheese, or fruit (when in season). Our particular favorite is the nalésniki ($2.50)—three rich, thin pancakes rolled around a cheese, jelly, or applesauce filling (you can select any combination). They are sauteed to a honey color and give us hunger pangs just thinking about them.

Other menu regulars include boiled beef accompanied by a mild horseradish sauce ($2.90) and tender roast chicken filled with a spicy bread dressing ($2.60). The Warsaw special ($3.50) includes some meats and some sweet. Your plate is filled to capacity with sausage, sauerkraut, stuffed cabbage, pierogi, and nalésniki. They make for strange neighbors, especially when tomato sauce starts moving into pancake territory. If potato pancakes happen to be on the menu, they're marvelous too.

All dinners at the Warsaw come with soup, bread, potato, vegetable, dessert and beverage. Try the czarnina (duck soup), a velvety blend filled with shell noodles, prunes, raisins, and just a hint of cinnamon. Sauerkraut soup is thick with shredded cabbage, and the beet soup brims with cabbage, carrots, onions and, of course, beets.

At the Warsaw you can dine downstairs, coffee-shop style or upstairs in a more lush dining room cum entertainment and a higher-priced menu on weekends.

# *Ana's Restaurant

2879 N. Elston
(at George Street, one block west of Western)
Phone: 486-9066
Parking: Street
No liquor

Mon.-Fri., 11:00 A.M.—8:30 P.M.
Closed Saturday, Sunday

Ana's is a cozy little corner restaurant serving the best Puerto Rican meals we've ever tasted. Everything about the place is guaranteed to put you in a good mood. The prices are incredibly low, each dish is under $1.75, and the people who work and eat here are extremely mellow. The menu is chalked up in Spanish, and the young, friendly waiters will be more than happy to explain it to you. They kind of bop around the place, mix in with the customers, and take an active interest in whether or not you're digging the food. Service is fast, especially around noon, when the place is packed with workers from the nearby factories.

The brief menu changes daily and features a variety of interesting Puerto Rican specialties, all prepared from scratch. Rellenos (35¢) are deep fried mashed potato balls filled with ground meat. They're delicious and not at all greasy. Alcapurrias (35¢) are green banana shells stuffed with ground meat and deep-fried, and pastelillos (40¢) are pastry turnovers, usually filled with chopped pork. There's guisado de pollo (chicken stew, $1.35), an outstanding blend of whole pieces of chicken, potatoes, green peppers, and green olives in a savory sauce. Other choices are a luscious beef stew ($1.50), pork chops and fried bananas ($1.65), and beef steak served with salad, bananas, or french fries ($1.65). Rice, which takes on new dimensions at Ana's, and abichuela (50¢), a bean-sausage-potato soup, round out the menu. The cook occasionally makes dessert, and his bread pudding (20¢ a serving) is excellent.

Small, sunny, and cheerful, Ana's is a fine place to sample generally unfamiliar and often maligned Puerto Rican cooking.

# Martingayle's

1820 N. Wells
Phone: 664-4562
Parking: Street
Full bar

Daily, 11:00 A.M.—2:00 A.M.
Sat., 11:00 A.M.—3:00 A.M.

Finding a good, relatively cheap seafood restaurant in Chicago is no easy task, but Martingayle's comes closest. Although we feel their bouillabaisse poses no threat for Marseilles, and their frog legs have hopped a bit too long, for price and overall quality, Martingayle's is a quite acceptable Chicago seafood spot. Located at the north end of Old Town, the place is generally filled with a young crowd. Its long series of rooms are done up in a nautical theme, with ship models, harpoons, and seascapes.

Most dinners, which include salad or slaw and cottage fries, cost under $4.00. However, if you add a soup, a side dish of hushpuppies and honey, or dessert, the price will be closer to $5.00.

The black clam chowder is well flavored with just a hint of curry, but you'll need a microscope to spot the clams, and we don't feel it's quite worth the [illegible]0¢ price. There's a nice broiled red snapper ($3.95), baked turbot in a sweet-sour sauce ($2.95), and catfish with hushpuppies ($3.50). The captain's platter ($4.95) contains a varied sampling—juicy shrimp, oysters, baked clams, frog legs, fried fish, and some unusual, tasty crab cakes. The clams are particularly delectable, baked in the shell with a garlicky, buttery bread crumb topping. The Alaskan king crab legs ($4.50) are generally firm and fresh-tasting. The freshness of the lobster ($6.95) cannot be doubted, as the luckless crustaceans can be observed moving about blissfully in a fish tank a la Dominick's. For those who are not partial to seafood, Martingayle's offers hamburgers and steaks.

Also, there's an excellent $3.95 per person Sunday brunch from 11 A.M. to 3 P.M., which features a bevy of sea delicacies such as lox and trimmings, caviar, lobster salad, herring, and smoked fish, plus eggs cooked to order, sweet rolls, and coffee.

# Slicker Sam's

1911 Rice Street,
Melrose Park
Phone: 345-5368
Parking: Street
Beer and wine

Daily, 11:00 A.M.—11:15 P.M.
Fri.-Sat., 11:00 A.M.—1:15 P.M.

Slicker Sam's is a noisy, informal, "roll up your sleeves and dig in" kind of place that serves some great seafood at prices worth the trip to Melrose Park. People come here to gorge. Posted on the wall, the menu is loaded with shellfish—shrimp, conch, crab, oysters, etc. Clams come raw ($2.50), steamed ($2.75), or baked in their shells ($3.25). The buttery, bread-crumb-topped baked oysters ($4.25) are fantastic, and raw oysters ($3.25) are here for the gulping. Large solid shrimp ($3.25) are done up nicely in a garlic-tarragon-flavored butter sauce. There's a hefty steamed crab, but priced out of our reach at $6.50.

Slicker Sam's also presents a bevy of pasta dishes—spaghetti and meat balls ($2.00), mostaciolli ($2.00), ravioli ($3.00), and lasagna ($4.25). They're all rather ordinary, topped with a far too powerful tomato sauce. You'll fare better with the linguine and clam sauce ($3.00). The minced clams are plentiful, and the sauce is a light butter-garlic.

There's pizza too. It has a medium-thick, crispy crust, mild sauce, ample cheese, and fresh-tasting extra ingredients ($2.85 for medium cheese and sausage). Eggplant parmigiana is equally well-prepared ($2.50).

Artichoke lovers will be in their glory at Slicker Sam's as the cooks do wondrous things with the vegetable. It is stuffed Italian-style with bread crumbs, herbs, and parmesan, then doused with butter and baked ($1.50). The antipasto doesn't come off as well, and it's $3.00 price is too high for its size.

Slicker Sam's is very popular and generally packed, so you may have to wait in line to get in. Prices are a la carte, and the bill can run up rapidly if you're not careful.

Directions: Take Eisenhower Expressway to 1st Avenue. Take 1st north to Lake. Left on Lake to Broadway and then turn right to Slicker Sam's.

# Gladys' Luncheonette

4527 S. Indiana
Phone: 548-6848
Parking: Street
No liquor

Daily, 24 hours
Closed Monday

The soul food here is some of the best in the city. Filling meals can be had for well under $3.00, sometimes even under $2.00. And the baker has a magic touch—biscuits and corn muffins are the best ever, feather-light and out-of-the-oven fresh.

Besides countless breakfasts and some sandwiches, Gladys' offers about ten dinners which include soup, two side dishes, and biscuits or cornbread. Dessert is extra. Chicken, needless to say, is fantastic. You can have it either fried or smothered in gravy for $1.60. For a truly gigantic meal, try the turkey wing and dressing ($2.25). The meat is so tender that it falls off the bone, the gravy is mellow, and the dressing is delicious—moist, spicy, and crumbly. Other choices can include smothered pork chops ($2.80), chicken livers and rice ($1.85), breaded perch ($2.25), and beef stew ($1.95).

For side dishes, you can stuff yourself on terrific fried corn, steamed cabbage, blackeyed peas, sweet potatoes, strong collard greens, rice, or spaghetti.

You will become nothing but fat and sassy on Gladys' desserts. There are two juicy cobblers, apple and peach (40¢), sweet potato pie (40¢), stewed apples (40¢), and strawberry shortcake (50¢). If you can't find room, be sure and take some home with you. In fact everything at Gladys' can be ordered to carry out and lots of people do just that.

Gradys' is open twenty-four hours, and it's liable to be crowded at any time.

# H & H Restaurant

1425 W. 87th
Phone: 445-4888
Parking: Lot
No liquor

Daily, 24 hours

For years H & H Cafe on East 51st Street was one of the most popular restaurants on the South Side. When it burned down a couple of years ago, owner Hubert Maybell decided not to mess around. He moved out to 87th Street and opened up a gigantic restaurant specializing in "soul smorgasboard".

The long table is laid out with a fabulous spread: all kinds of salads (macaroni, three bean, tossed, potato, slaw, pickled corn), candied yams, mashed potatoes, spaghetti, creamed corn, okra, turnip greens, smothered chicken, fried chicken, ham hocks, rib tips, fried catfish, and everyone's favorite—chitterlings. To fill you further, there are flaky biscuits, fantastic buttery corn muffins on a par with Gladys', peach cobbler, apple cobbler, and, sometimes, vanilla tarts. Though everything's good, the sweet-sauced ribs are something else, and the fried chicken's not far behind.

You'll eat till you can't move, and all for prices that are more than kind. The buffet costs $2.95 from 11:00 A.M. until 3:00 P.M. From 3:00 P.M. til 2:00 A.M. it escalates to $3.30. Sunday smorgasbord stays at $3.50 all day. And kids under twelve will set you back only $1.75.

The H & H is spotless, and all the staff is very friendly. You just walk in, grab a plate and fill it up. Carry-outs are available too.

# Soul Queen Café

2200 S. Michigan
Phone: 842-0298
Parking: Street
No liquor

Daily, 24 hours

Helen C. Maybell operates a twenty-four-hour eating emporium specializing in soul food. One of her avowed purposes is to expose soul food to the general public, and she really does her restaurant up right. A friendly hostess seats you and keeps in touch with how you're doing, the booths are comfortable, and some good sounds drift through the room. The whole atmosphere is geared to please, right down to the optimistic, fortune-cookie-like message pasted on each napkin.

The menu features many traditional dishes, all very decently priced. There are ham hocks ($2.50), catfish ($2.60), buffalo fish ($2.50), and southern fried chicken ($2.50). The deep-fried catfish is flaky and fresh-tasting. The fried chicken is golden and crusty on the outside and moist inside. Some of the daily specials include stewed chicken and dumplings ($2.50) on Thursdays, and chitterlings ($3.00) on Saturdays.

All meals feature delicious piping hot corn bread sticks, two side dishes, and dessert. We liked the red pepper-laced greens and the nutmeg-flavored candied yams best. Dessert is generally a spicy peach cobbler, although sometimes there's also yam pie.

Soul Queen Café is a great place to sample some first-rate soul cooking.

# Costa Brava

4006 N. Broadway
Phone: 929-5510
348-8796
Parking: Street
B.Y.O.

Daily, 11:00 A.M.—11:00 P.M.
Closed Tuesday

Costa Brava is a tiny, almost-hidden storefront restaurant that serves up some very imaginative Latin food. Where else can you get a dish called "old clothes" (ropa vieja) or a spicy shrimp, crab leg, octopus, clam-studded fish soup for only $2.50? The Cuban-born owner, Carlos Perez, followed the advice of friends who urged him on with the proverbial "you cook so well, you ought to open a restaurant." We think they were justified, because Mr. Perez's cooking is both distinctive and delicious. It's possible to eat well here for under $4.00, though extras can pad your bill.

Entrees, which are accompanied by hot French bread, include several far from mundane choices. One of particular interest is lomo saltado ($4.75), a blend of sauteed beef, potatoes, onions, and tomatoes. It's served with rice and either a tasty salad or two anticuchos (marinated beef hearts). Bistek Costa Brava ($3.75) is New York cut steak fried with chopped onions and Cuban bananas. The bananas are unbelievably good—thick, sweet, crisp outside and soft inside. It's also possible to order a side of bananas for 30¢. Two other beef dishes are cacerole steak ($2.75), a stew of beef, green peppers, onions, and tomatoes, and the aforementioned ropa vieja ($2.50), shredded beef in a green pepper-garlic-tomato sauce.

Arroz con pollo ($2.75) is presented in a portion big enough to feed the entire Chicago police force. However, Mr. Perez's true triumph, paella, comes under the splurge category. For $6.70 per person, you can feast on the most seafood-decorated paella we've ever seen. It's brimming with lobster, king crab legs, shrimp, clams, mussels, octopus, and chicken atop a bed of saffron rice.

Costa Brava serves some traditional desserts, including our favorite, guayaba (guava) with cream cheese (70¢), a smooth flan (60¢), and rice pudding (60¢).

# *Ann Sather's

925 W. Belmont
Phone: 348-2378
Parking: Street
No liquor

Daily, 11:00 A.M.—8:00 P.M.
Sunday, Noon—7:00 P.M. (Menu prices slightly higher)

If your favorite fantasy centers on fresh-baked bread and pyramids of pies and puddings, Ann Sather's will fulfill it. With its immaculate, cheerful, tearoom sort of charm, it is the brightest spot on a dreary stretch of Belmont Avenue, and we love it. Knicknacks are everywhere, and decorations change with the season. Service is exceptionally friendly and fast (especially if you get Maud, Doris, or Betty), food quality is impeccable, and prices remarkably low. Complete dinners include soup, bread, salad, entree, two side dishes, beverage, and dessert.

Bread comes first, and what bread it is—thick, fluffy white bread, banana-nut bread, perhaps a gooey caramel roll, or candied orange peel-studded limpa bread. All but the limpa are freshly made in Ann's kitchen.

For an appetizer, we suggest the Swedish cold fruit soup (fresh and dried fruit in cinnamon-spiced raspberry juice) or any soup of lentil, pea, or vegetable origin.

Entrees vary each day. Try the moist, tender, baked chicken ($3.15), any of the pot pies (around $2.65), or the very tasty Swedish meatballs (2.80). There's also roast pork or lamb ($3.60), swiss steak ($4.00), or maybe a strawberry or peach omelette (2.85). Side dishes are very nice: super-sweet Swedish brown beans, home-made applesauce, sweet and sour cole slaw, German potato salad, or some great candied squash if it's in season. Meat portions aren't huge, but once you make your way through the side dishes your ability to go on is threatened.

No matter how stuffed you feel, dessert is a must. Sather's makes the best homemade pies ever: strawberry-banana with homemade whipped cream, almond cream, banana cream, apricot-prune, fresh plum, and many more. Puddings—Indian, rice, spice, or apple Brown Betty—are fine too.

Lunch is equally good here. Try the hot Swedish meatball sandwich ($1.35) or the paper-thin Swedish pancakes with lingonberries ($1.35).

# Villa Sweden

5207 N. Clark
Phone: 334-1883
Parking: Street
No Liquor

Daily, 11:00 A.M.—8:30 P.M.
Smorgasbord:
Thursday, 4:00 P.M.—8:00 P.M.
Friday, 11:00 A.M.—2:30 P.M.
Sunday, 11:30 A.M.—8:00 P.M.

Located in the Andersonville neighborhood, Villa Sweden offers Scandinavian cooking at its best. With its deep blue and white color scheme, the dining room offers a sedate, restful atmosphere. Waitresses dress in costume and are pleasant and efficient.

The big attraction at Villa Sweden is its elaborate smorgasbord ($4.00 per person; children, $2.50), which, together with Mategrano's, is the best in the city. No one could possibly leave hungry.

Food is artistically arranged, with cold and hot dishes being kept at their proper temperatures. The selections are varied, and the supply seems endless. There are several cold meats and a variety of salads: herring, cucumber salad, pickled beets. Hawaiian fruit salad, thin-sliced ham, salami, delicious corn beef, and hopefully—the true beauty—a whole, poached salmon. There are chafing dishes of roast chicken, Swedish meatballs, sweet brown beans, and a surprisingly tasty spaghetti. A smooth custard with raspberry sauce and fruit compote comprise the dessert selection.

Beverage, limpa bread, and sweet tea bread are served at the table. You're actually encouraged to eat as much as you want, and each time you go up to the buffet table, the waitress clears your old plate. It all reminds you of a good dream.

On non-buffet nights, the complete dinners aren't too hard to take, either. Priced in the $2.75 to $3.75 range, they begin with a choice of soup or juice, and include salad, potato, vegetable, entree, dessert, and beverage. Some recommended offerings are the Swedish meatballs, baked chicken with lingonberries, and the baked ham.

# *Bangkok House

2544 W. Devon Avenue
Phone: 338-5948
Parking: Street
B.Y.O.

Daily, 4:00 P.M.—10:00 P.M.
Fri., 4:00 P.M.—Midnight
Sat., 11:00 A.M.—Midnight
Sun., 11:00 A.M.—10:00 P.M.
Closed Tuesday

If you savor hot, fiery food redolent with curry and hot pepper, Thai food is for you and prepared to perfection at Bangkok House. However, Bangkok House also features many dishes similar to and no more potent than those found in Cantonese restaurants. Tell Ms. Limphaibulc, the owner and hostess, how adventurous you feel, and she will guide you accordingly.

Ease your way gently by sampling one of the marvelous appetizers: fresh, crisply fried wonton ($1.25), delicious vegetable-stuffed eggroll ($1.25), or chicken or beef satay (skewered grilled meat, served with curry sauce, $1.25).

Particularly recommended among the peppery dishes are chicken with red peppers and cashews ($2.95), beef with hot peppers and green onions ($2.55), and chicken with Thai curry ($1.95). If you like your curry to walk on the mild side, the shrimp curry contains loads of firm shrimp, pineapple, and sauteed onion in a mild, pleasantly spiced sauce ($2.75).

Best of the non-spicy dishes is the savory sauteed chicken with young corn and black mushrooms ($2.55). The chicken shares a subtle sauce with black mushrooms, bamboo shoots, sweet onions, and a real delicacy, miniature corn on the cob. We found the roast duck, Thai-style, unenjoyable ($2.25), as the meat was too fatty and the sauce too salty. The sweet and sour dishes are filled with colorful ingredients, but are neither sweet nor sour enough and come in a tomato-soup-like sauce.

All entrees are accompanied by a large bowl of perfectly cooked rice (at a slight extra charge) and a pot of tea. For dessert, Thai pudding is in the "must try" category. It's an unusual but delectable combination of ground peas, sugar, and coconut milk topped with fried onions. Don't let these ingredients turn you off, because the silky, moist pudding is both refreshing and delicious.

# Bangkok Restaurant

3525 N. Halsted
Phone: 327-2870
Parking: Street
B.Y.O.

Daily, 10:00 A.M.—10:00 P.M.
Fri.-Sat., 10:00 A.M.—11:00 P.M.
Closed Monday

One of the newest and most authentic of the host of Thai restaurants which has appeared in the past couple of years is this comfortable corner storefront. Just about everything we've tried has been well-prepared, generous with ingredients, and interestingly seasoned. Prices are low enough to try a variety of dishes. As for the spiciness of the food, this is only one aspect of Thai cooking. There's plenty on the menu that everyone can enjoy.

Among the mild selections are delectably crisp, meat-filled, fried won ton ($1.50), sweet and sour chicken or shrimp (not batter-fried, $2.00 to $2.50), and a light, slightly sweet meatball soup with rice stick ($1.00 or $1.50).

The real jewel of the kitchen is charcoal chicken ($2.50), one of the best renditions of the bird we've ever eaten. Skin is crackly, the meat is moist and plump, and a delicious teriyaki-like marinade permeates all. It is served with a side of sweet apricot sauce. Other mild offerings include moist Korean rice filled with sprouts, chicken, shrimp, egg, peas, parsley, and shredded carrots ($2.00), and Thai barbequed pork ($1.00 to $1.50).

Some slightly hotter dishes worth a try are pan-fried ground beef and rice with mint ($1.75), and shrimp salad ($2.50), peppery charcoaled shrimp served on a bed of shredded lettuce. The hot shrimp soup ($2.50) is no misnomer—it clears out your sinuses and brings on a mild state of euphoria. It boasts firm fresh shrimp, button mushrooms, and a delicious lemony tang, but is absolutely the hottest thing around this side of the eggplant curry at Maharaja.

Desserts are unusual, but the ground bean pudding-cake (50¢) has an interesting texture and is quite good. There's a drink called mali (50¢) that's made from a Thai flower and would delight a hummingbird. Service is friendly and fast, but there is a language problem which is bound to improve as the waitresses become more familiar with non-Thai patrons.

# Siam Café

4654 N. Sheridan
Phone: 784-9580
Parking: Street
B.Y.O.

Daily, Noon—Midnight
Closed Monday

One of our favorite discoveries is this tiny Thai restaurant in Uptown. It is run by an amiable family who offer one of the lowest-priced Asian menus around. Only one item, sweet and sour shrimp at $2.50, is over $2.00. The feeling here is very homey. There's a big stack of Thai magazines near the entrance, and one evening we ate dinner to the accompaniment of *Tora! Tora! Tora!* on the TV.

The cuisine here is primarily Chinese with Thai overtones, making it milder than that found in other Thai restaurants. The exception is the zingy cucumber salad laced with jalapeno peppers which serves as a preliminary to each meal.

The food is priced low enough so that you can experiment with a variety of dishes. Particularly recommended is the Siam Bar B Q ($1.15), a half dozen small skewers of barbequed pork which comes with a dip of creamy peanut sauce (like a homemade peanut butter) The whole thing is slightly oily, but very delicious. There are egg rolls ($1.00), fried won ton ($1.00), and soups: won ton, beef, and ya ka mein (long, curly noodles, pork slices, and bean sprouts in a light broth.) Good-sized bowls cost $1.00.

The roast duck with rice ($1.50) makes an excellent entree. The skin is crisp and glazed with a teriyaki-like sauce, and the meat is succulent and juicy. Tomato-green pepper-beef ($2.00) or beef kai lan (thin strips of beef sauteed with Chinese broccoli and bean sprouts, $1.50) are other possibilities. Barbequed pork and rice ($1.00) is terrific: lean, thin-sliced pork in a semi-sweet red bean sauce. The colorful sweet and sour dishes contain fresh, crisp ingredients, but the meat is not batter-coated, and the sauce could use more zip. The menu also lists bargain-priced beef, chicken, pork, and shrimp chop suey, chow mein, and fried rice.

Please don't dip your fingers in the silver water bowls as we did. The bowls are for drinking.

# Siamese Restaurant

3961 N. Ashland
Phone: 248-6351
Parking: Street
B.Y.O.

Tue.-Thur., 4:00 P.M.—Midnight
Fri., 4:00 P.M.—2:00 A.M.
Sat., Noon—2:00 A.M.
Closed Monday

We've visited the Siamese Restaurant many times, and it always looks like it closed two weeks ago, or is perhaps two weeks away from opening. Don't let this disturb you. Its plain lackluster atmosphere belies a very imaginative cuisine. This is underscored by its popularity among young Thais who gather here by the groupful, particularly on weekend evenings.

Although about half the menu is made up of Chinese dishes, it is the Thai selections that command interest. By all means try the steamed mussels. For $2.95 you receive about three dozen large mussels in the shell, served in a tasty broth. A side dish of hot pepper sauce comes along for dunking. Thai barbequed pork ($1.55) is good too, and its accompanying peanut sauce is rich tasting, though oily.

Another highlight is the deep-fried whole red snapper ($3.95), served as either pla krapong num dang (in a mushroom-pork sauce) or pla lud nar prik (in a hot pepper-onion sauce). The latter is unnervingly hot, as it's literally bathed with fiery chopped peppers. Two other mouth-roasting but very tasty dishes are nua pud prik ($2.35), a beef, onion, and hot pepper combination and its close relative, chicken pud prik ($2.35, not on the menu).

To cool you down, there's a pale, flavorful fried rice ($1.75) and sen mee lud nar ($1.75), a pleasant blend of vermicelli noodles, beef, and greens. The two mild, meal-sized soups, tom yum kung (shrimp, $2.95) and tom yum kai (chicken, $2.35), contain a maze of curly noodles, a healthy portion of either shrimp or chicken, scallions, and greens.

A word about the plain rice. It is priced rather high at 50¢ per person, and one order is probably enough for two. Getting this across to whomever serves you may be difficult, however, and more than likely you'll end up paying 50¢ apiece anyway. Luckily, it's good rice.

# Sophie's

2132 W. Chicago
Phone: 252-9625
Parking: Street
No liquor

Daily, Noon—10:00 P.M.

Sophie's is a simple, immaculate, Mom-and-Pop-run restaurant in the old Ukrainian neighborhood on Chicago Avenue. Everything in the small dining room looks like it's been polished with a toothbrush. Owners John and Sophie have been at their Chicago Avenue location for thirteen years, and still seem to enjoy what they're doing. While offering you a glass of "Lake Michigan Champagne," John usually will get a conversation going about prices, politics, or conditions in Chicago. In the meantime, good things are happening in the kitchen.

All meals include soup, and are super-bargain priced between $2.00 and $2.10. And it's all honest, nothing-fancy cooking. Soups are made from scratch and vary each day. There's a slightly sour sauerkraut soup filled with shredded cabbage, carrots, giblets, and bacon bits, a beet soup, potato soup, mushroom-noodle, or an unusual, refreshing cold apple soup.

The entrees are generally limited to four. If you like dumplings, Pyrohy are usually available, filled with cheese, potatoes, sauerkraut, or blueberries (in season.) The beef stew has that homemade touch and the meat can be cut with a fork. It comes with a mushroom-flavored gravy, boiled potato, salad, and a canned vegetable. The slightly spicy, loaf-shaped meatballs are quite tasty. Pork tenderloin, roast chicken, or perhaps duck ($2.50) may also be among the offerings. All come with vegetable, potato, and salad.

# Gale Street Inn

4914 N. Milwaukee
Phone: 283-9499
Parking: Street
Full bar

Daily, 11:00 A.M.—1:00 A.M.
(kitchen hours)
Closed Monday

The original Gale Street Inn was torn down to make way for the Jefferson Park Rapid Transit depot. Fortunately, it relocated directly across the street with a sleek new image.

For years Gale Street has had a local reputation for its hamburgers, beef sandwiches, and what many consider to be the best ribs in the city. With its glossy new character, the menu has enlarged considerably to include six reasonably-priced steaks plus such current menu regulars as french fried mushrooms and "surf and turf". However, the oldies are still the goodies.

The ribs are so tender that the meat falls off the bone, and the portion is enormous. They are well-glazed with a nippy barbeque sauce and decently priced at $4.95, which includes baked potato and a crouton-topped salad. The butt steak sandwich ($3.25) is a good-sized, tasty piece of beef, served on black rye. Hamburgers ($1.90) are thick, and the juicy roast beef sandwich ($2.00) is excellent. All sandwiches come with a dentist-sized cupful of slaw and some unexciting french fries. (We recommend avoiding a side of mushroom caps or onion rings, as both identities are difficult to discover beneath the heavy breading.)

Gale Street is apt to be packed, but lines move swiftly. The decor is suburban rec room, with bar-sized statues of Laurel and Hardy, team pennants, plus two real treasures—baseball bats autographed by Ron Santo and Mr. Cub.

# The Hamburger King

3435 N. Sheffield
Phone: 281-4452
Parking: Street
No liquor

Daily, 6 A.M.—Midnight
Closed Sunday

If you're down to your last dollar and spare change, and in need of a nourishing meal, Hamburger King is the place to go. The food isn't glorious and some things are best left alone, but the price is definitely right.

Hamburger King is a gathering place for locals of all ages and persuasions. The decor is funky, and seating can be had at either a long, curving counter or at a few tables. The Japanese cooks do a commendable short-order job, considering the variety on the menu. All dinners come with soup (served only till 8:00 P.M.), bread, entree, vegetable, and potato or rice. Prices go as low as 90¢ for a cheese omelette and up to $2.10 for the grilled pork chop dinner.

If you happen upon the barley soup, it's fairly rich and quite tasty. Grilled liver and onions ($1.35) are very nice, and the hamburger steak with fried onions isn't bad either. There are a few Chinese dishes on the menu, such as a tasty Yet Ka Mein (noodle soup) and Egg Foo Young. The Egg Fu Young tastes fresh, is heavy on bean sprouts, and three large patties cost only $1.15 on the dinner. Ask them to hold back the gravy because it's not the soy-molasses type, but the same kind used on the regular meat dishes.

Hamburger King is not for the gourmet, but among greasy spoons it has few peers.

# Homestead

12126 S. Vincennes, Blue Island
Phone: 385-2570
Parking: Lot
Full bar

Tue.-Thur., 4:30 P.M.—12:30 A.M.
Fri.-Sat., 4:30 P.M.—1.30 A.M.
Sun., 1:00 P.M.—10:30 P.M.
Closed Monday

Everyone goes to the Homestead for their barbequed ribs. The full slab is almost two feet long while the regular is not much smaller. The ribs are meaty, tender babybacks with a great hickory-smoked flavor that permeates both the meat and the sauce. The only problem is that—ribs being ribs—they cost well over $4.50: the full slab is $6.25 and the regular $5.75. However, for quality, taste, and size they're worth a splurge.

The rib dinner includes family-style servings of relishes, kidney bean salad, cottage cheese, and tossed salad with a very potent garlic dressing. It all tastes good—even the cottage cheese. Rolls and either french fries or a baked potato complete the meal.

It's also possible to enjoy a full dinner at the Homestead for under $4.50, but only if you don't like ribs. The barbequed half chicken costs $3.50, and is moist, tender, and covered with the same delicious sauce as the ribs. The pan-fried chicken or the deep-fried chicken are also good. In addition, the menu includes a selection of steaks and a fine prime rib (weekends only) that are decently priced and sized, but well over our budget.

The Homestead's continued growth and success can be measured by its many additions, extending from the original tavern-like building out to the newest link, which could easily pass for a pancake house. The interior all holds together in brightly lit, early American. The place is generally swarming, particularly on weekends.

Directions: Take the Dan Ryan Expressway south to I-57. Take 127th St. exit, turn right about 1 mile to Vincennes. Turn right on Vincennes to the Homestead.

# Jay's Campus Cafe

832 Foster,
Evanston
Phone: 475-9568
Parking: Street
No liquor

Tue.-Fri., 11:30 A.M.—12:30 A.M.
Sat., 4:30 P.M.—12:30 A.M.
Sun., 4:30 P.M.—10:30 P.M.

Not too many strides from Northwestern, Jay's looks and feels like many a campus restaurant. But one thing makes it different—the food is good. Jay's trim menu features eleven specials, most of which are served with two side dishes, and the portions are heaping.

One of the most bountiful selections is the chef's salad ($1.95), a mountainous mix of lettuce, ham, chicken, swiss cheese, hard boiled egg, tomato, asparagus, shredded carrots, and onion, all of which can be topped by a fresh-tasting thousand island dressing (or garlic, French, oil and vinegar.) Our other favorite is the steak kabob ($2.25), cubes of charcoaled beef, green pepper, and onion served on French bread with a scrumptious, messy barbeque sauce. Also you can't go wrong with the hamburger ($1.40) or the barbequed chicken ($2.55).

If none of these do it, there's beef stew served on corn-bread ($3.00), a corned beef sandwich ($1.90), stuffed peppers ($2.10), bratwurst ($1.50), a huge bowl of beef-vegetable soup ($1.95 or 85¢ for a smaller version), a cheese and French bread plate ($2.40), and omelettes ($1.40 for a plain, up to $1.70 for a Denver).

Side dishes are mostly starchy, filling, and good. You can choose your two from among potato salad, baked beans, baked potato, corn bread, and cole slaw. Our only complaint is the papaya juice (30¢), which tasted more like the orange drink at Walgreens. Hot cider with cinnamon is delicious, though.

# R. J. Grunt's

2056 Lincoln Park West
Phone: 929-5363
Parking: Street (difficult)
Full bar

Daily, 11:30 A.M.—Midnight
Fri.-Sat., 11:30 A.M.—1:00 A.M.

R. J. Grunt's can herd you around like cattle and ply you with expensive, exotic (but delicious) drinks, but we'll keep coming back for more. More, that is, of their lavish salad bar, probably the best in town. For $2.75 you can stuff yourself on herring, excellent chopped liver, caviar, 3-bean salad, tossed lettuce salad, cole slaw, a wheel of cheese, and an incredible array of fresh fruit (pineapple, cantelope, plums, pears, cherries—whatever's in season,) and more. It's truly Bacchanalian and not to be missed. The luncheon salad bar costs $1.67, but the offerings are much more limited.

Grunt's gimmicky, complicated menu reads about as easily as a cryptogram. It's geared to please all of the people all of the time. There's vegetarian spaghetti ($1.85) and sirloin steak ($6.95), steamed shrimp ($3.75), Dungeness crab ($5.75) and a "love omelette" ("sauteed eggplant . . . nestled lovingly into freshly beaten eggs"). All dinners automatically include a trip to the salad bar and a mini-loaf of bread.

Best bets, however, are the sandwiches. Our favorite is the barbeque beef (thin-sliced, juicy brisket) with fried onions and cottage fries, the hamburger or cheeseburger (both $2.10), or a crisp veal cutlet, melted cheese and tomato sauce conglomeration ($2.05). One dollar will buy you salad with your sandwich. But resist the tempting but we think ripoff-priced fruit juices (85¢) and milk shakes ($1.25).

There's a singles-bar feel and crush to Grunt's, but the mirrors, high ceiling, and bigger-than-life paintings make the room seem larger than it is. Waitresses are young and generally friendly.

### *FRITZ, THAT'S IT*

1615 Chicago Avenue Evanston
Phone: 866-8506

Son of Grunt's. Same as above, only more so.

# St. Regis Hotel

520 N. Clark
Phone: 467-1235
Parking: Street
Full Bar

Daily: 6:00 A.M.—2:00 A.M.
Sun., Noon—2:00 A.M.

The St. Regis is an offbeat place located on what remains of Clark Street's skid row. You enter the dining room through a bar filled with men who look like extras from *The Man With the Golden Arm*. After the street and the bar, you're not prepared for the dining room. It's quite elaborate with dark paneling, sumptuous booths, red linen tablecloths, and subtle lighting.

One look at the extensive menu, and you can see that the St. Regis offers bargains to rival those of the ethnic restaurants. Complete dinners, including appetizer, beverage, and dessert, average $3.00.

Appetizers range from soup (barley, chicken noodle, vegetable, etc.) to chopped liver or herring. A decent, standard salad is next. Entrees vary daily and might include roast pork loin with dressing ($3.25), fried liver with onions or bacon ($2.75), breaded veal cutlet and spaghetti ($2.05), roast turkey with trimmings ($2.85), and eggplant parmigiana ($2.75). All are tastily prepared, and the tender, crisply fried liver is exceptional. Vegetables and potatoes are served with dinner, including a good quality baked potato with sour cream. There are also several seafood selections (including scallops, oysters, and whitefish) priced under $3.00, all of which come with salad and potatoes.

Desserts go beyond the usual jello and ice cream to a choice of sundaes, layer cakes, pudding, or half a grapefruit.

Though there are no gourmet pretenses about the St. Regis, its kitchen assures you a meal that is both simple and well-prepared.

# Balkan at Night

3446 N. Pulaski
Phone: 283-0403
Parking: Street
Full bar

Tue.-Fri., 4:00 P.M.—2:00 A.M.
Sat., 4:00 P.M.—3:00 A.M.
Sun., 1:00 P.M.—2:00 A.M.

The candlelit tables, thick, deep rose-colored curtains, and massive Oriental rugs on the walls of Balkan at Night create a feeling of mystery and intrigue. But, alas, no Bela Lugosi. Instead an enticing selection of Serbian specialties await you.

Main course, plus salad and bread, averages $3.50. All dishes are beautifully arranged and presented, and portions are large.

Experiment with the delicious cevapcici ($3.50), tiny, grilled homemade sausages with a subtle spicy flavor. The equally good shish kebab ($3.75) is made of fork-tender chunks of grilled pork tenderloin. A combination plate of cevapcici and shish kebab ($3.50) is a good compromise. Muckalica ($4.50) contains a flavorful, stew-like blend of bite-sized pork tenderloin, mushrooms, onions, green peppers, and tomatoes. Pljeskavica ($3.75) is a somewhat coarse-textured chopped steak containing bits of onion and green pepper. Hungarian beef goulash and liver and onions are also available. Daily specials include an interesting musaka ($3.50) on Wednesdays. It's made of ground beef, veal, and pork, cooked between layers of potatoes and either eggplant or cauliflower. If you have a few extra dollars in your pocket, try the Serbian hot plate ($10 for two), a mammoth platter piled with grilled pork chops, veal, liver, cevapcici, lamb chops, and more.

Each entree is served with one of the most interesting and artistically arranged salads around. It includes a tangy marinated cole slaw in addition to tossed greens, tomatoes, feta cheese, and pickled beets.

Desserts are priced rather high at 80¢. The slice of apple strudel is large and looks much better than it tastes.

Though Balkan at Night may seem quiet during the week, it really comes alive on weekend evenings after 10:00 P.M. when there's spirited entertainment (and a twenty per cent cover charge).

# The Bowl and Roll

1246 N. Wells
Phone: 943-1437
Parking: Street (difficult)
Full bar

Daily, 11:30 A.M.—10:30 P.M.
Fri.-Sat., 11:30 A.M.—Midnight
Sun., 11:30 A.M.—10:00 P.M.
Closed Monday

The Bowl and Roll is a super little soup house and easily the best budget restaurant in Old Town. The menu features three kinds of nourishing soup, all beautifully prepared and served with hot, crusty Toscana bread. These stew-like soups are meals in themselves, and the menu doesn't lie when it says they cannot be finished with a spoon.

The chicken soup (¼ chicken, $1.25; ½ chicken, $1.75) is a fresh, light medley of garden vegetables, noodles, and tender whole pieces of chicken. It's similar to the Jewish specialty, chicken-in-the-pot, and probably just as good a cure-all. Goulash soup ($2.00) is a heavier affair—rich, thick with big chunks of meat, a weighty dumpling, and vegetables. It's worth coming in out of the cold for. The unusual bean soup ($2.00) rounds out the triumverate. It's pleasantly flavored with sour cream and either a ham hock (slightly fatty) or a potent Hungarian sausage.

If you'd like some greenery to go with your soup, the house salad (75¢) with its Green-Goddess-like dressing, is better than average. The poached salmon in champagne mayonnaise ($2.00) turns out to be a glorified salmon salad, though much better than the kind you probably ate as a kid. There are also three sandwiches—a tasty chopped liver, Hungarian sausage, and cheese.

Desserts are simple. Many people rave about the raisin-pecan brownie (one night we saw a man carry out three dozen,) but we were somewhat disappointed. They are a little dry, and at 50¢ apiece, too high-priced. The deep-dish apple pie (50¢) is tasty, especially when topped by a scoop of Vala's ice cream (25¢).

Bowl and Roll takes some sleuthing to spot—it's set back from the sidewalk and there's only a small sign. Nestled in the former Cave restaurant, the atmosphere is snug and comfortable; service is fast, but you're welcome to linger.

# Ratso's

2464 N. Lincoln
Phone: 935-1505
Parking: Street
Full bar

Dinner: Daily, 5:00 P.M.—12:30 A.M. (or thereabouts)
Buffet: Tue., Wed., Thur., 5:00 P.M.—8:00 P.M.
Sunday Brunch: 11:30 A.M.—3:30 P.M. (get there early)

No once can accuse Ratso's of not being open to change. It has one of the most diverse menus around and is always willing to experiment with something new. Who else has tried Sunday brunches with live chamber music? One of their most popular innovations is the Wednesday night buffet which has recently expanded to include Tuesday and Thursday (call ahead to make sure). It's an all-you-can-eat-for-$2.75 extravaganza featuring an international melting pot of foods. The array boggles the mind: tamale pie, veal stroganoff, lasagne, chicken teriyaki, moussaka, fried rice, baked beans, quiche lorraine, German potato pancakes, Greek lamb, and batter fried eggplant, not to mention tossed salad, slaw, potato salad, macaroni salad, and a variety of canapes.

Though Ratso's kitchen can be erratic and quality can vary with the disposition or talent of the cook, the buffet generally offers several fine dishes. Among the best are the crisp fried eggplant, the juicy chicken teriyaki, and the custard-topped moussaka. The quiche has a nice addition of spinach and even tastes great cold, which it just might be. There's plenty to eat and plenty of time to do it in.

Don't overlook Ratso's appealing if bizarre regular menu with everything from chicken Kiev to some vegetarian things like Ratso Rizzo, a fried rice, onion, green pepper, mushroom, and sunflower seed combination.

The crowd at Ratso's is mixed, particularly on buffet night, with young, middle-aged, families, and singles. The dining room is big, brick, and somewhat cheerless, and waitresses range from friendly to forgetful. There's good live jazz, blues, folk, or rock music every night from around 9 P.M. on.

# Splurges

# The Bakery

2218 N. Lincoln
Phone: 472-6942
Parking: Street (difficult)
Wine served
Credit Cards: None accepted

Tue.-Thur., 5:00 P.M.—11:00 P.M.
Fri.-Sat., 5:00 P.M.—Midnight
Closed Sunday, Monday
Reservations necessary

The Bakery and its flamboyant owner-chef, Louis Szathmáry, seem to have achieved the status of Chicago institution, joining the mayor, Len O'Conner and the 16″ softball. If you order the right dishes, and if you aren't hurried, dining here can be a most satisfying experience, even though complete five-course dinners are now up to a stiff $11.00.

The paté, served with slivered dill pickles and Toscana bread, gets you off to a fantastic start, while soups are a work of art. Among the best are cauliflower, asparagus, and a lemon-flavored tomato that is so good it ought to make Campbell's blush. The salad which follows is a pleasant blend of fresh greens, hardboiled eggs, herbs, and a creamy, slightly sweet dressing.

Our favorite among the entrees is the ever-reliable roast duck with cherry sauce. The portion is big, the meat succulent, and, while the sauce may be slightly sweet for some, we find it delicious. Beef Wellington is expertly prepared and very rich. If beef or veal stroganoff or Szekely goulash are on the menu, all are consistently good. We have been disappointed by other offerings, particularly the fish.

Side dishes are outstanding, as The Bakery has a rare touch with vegetables. Red cabbage, carrots with dilled cream sauce, and ratatouille are all delicious. So are the desserts, particularly the sumptuous banana eclair with custard and chocolate brandy sauce.

The restaurant is housed in a series of simple yet charming rooms, and the feeling is quite homey. A few drawbacks: tables are cramped together and service, although excellent, can be rushed. At any rate, if you've eaten at The Bakery you probably have a definite opinion. If not, we think the food is still among the best in the city.

# *The Blackhawk

139 N. Wabash
Phone: 726-0100
Parking: Free lot at Randolph and Wabash
Full bar
Credit Cards: American Express, Bank America, Carte Blanche, Diners Club, Master Charge

Mon.-Fri., 11:00 A.M.—10:30 P.M.
Sat., 11:00 A.M.—1:00 P.M.
Sun., 3:30 P.M.—10:30 P.M.

When Uncle Joe from Kearney, Nebraska comes to town, head him toward The Blackhawk, downtown Chicago's most reliable restaurant. The place is sure to please for its smoothly professional service (with an added bit of flourish), comfortable seating, and fine quality all-American fare. The menu is weighted with beef and portions are lavish.

All meals begin with garlic-buttered, toasty party rye, which proves to be habit-forming and inevitably vanishes quickly. The restaurant's tour de force, the Blackhawk salad, is next. The legend of the spinning salad bowl is right up there among the best, and we never tire of the waiter's recitation as he tosses the salad "just six times so as not to bruise the tender greens." Its fame is justified as its one of the best salads around—an enormous, tangy medley of crisp lettuce, chopped eggs, bleu cheese, "secret" Blackhawk dressing, herbs, and optional anchovies.

For an entree, the carved to order roast prime rib ($7.45) is the house specialty. The meat could win a contest on its looks alone, and, happily, its appearance is not deceiving. It's as succulent and flavorful as any beef we've ever eaten. If you'd like a bone to chew, order the prime rib with bone ($8.25). Be sure to request the delicious whipped cream-horseradish sauce to go along with it.

Although prime rib is as important to The Blackhawk as Mikita is to the Blackhawks, you can also count on an excellent steak ($7.35 to $8.50). If you feel like deviating further, try the scrod. It's shipped in each day from a Boston fish market, and it's exceedingly fresh and sweet. Baked potato with sour cream and chives and delectable creamed spinach are perfect accompaniments to the entrees.

# The Casbah

514 W. Diversey
Phone: 935-7570
Free garage parking
Full bar
Credit Cards: Bank of America, Carte Blanche, Diners Club, Master Charge

Mon.-Thur., 5:30 P.M.—11:30 P.M.
Fri.-Sat., 5:30 P.M.—Midnight
Sun., 5:30 P.M.—10:30 P.M.
Reservations necessary

The Casbah with its dramatic, soft lighting, murals of veiled women and palm trees, ornate hanging lanterns, and carved arches, is the most exotic of our splurges. It conjures visions of Charles Boyer and Hedy Lamarr among the minarets. The food, while less theatrical, is nonetheless unusual and delicious.

Dinners cost between $5.00 and $7.00 and include appetizer, egg-lemon soup, salad, entree, and either American or Turkish coffee. While both of the dinner appetizers—hommos (ground chick pea spread) and djadic (a tart mix of cucumbers, yogurt, and mint) are excellent, be sure to try the beorak (60¢ extra). It's a combination of cheese, parsley and onions baked sizzling hot in a parchment thin strudel dough.

Among the Armenian entrees are four variations on the shish kabab, with the Armenian kabab ($6.50) being our preference. Tender marinated lamb is alternately skewered between eggplant, green pepper, tomatoes, and onions. Rice pilaf is served with all of the kababs. Two other top choices are meat beorak, chopped meat, onions, and tomatoes wrapped in strudel dough ($5.75) and maglube, a tasty casserole of well-seasoned rice, lamb cubes, cauliflower, and pinenuts ($5.50, served only on weekends). Kibbe (deep fried balls of cracked wheat, ground lamb, onions, and walnuts, $5.65) and sarma (stuffed grape leaves, $5.50) are two other possibilities.

For dessert, baklava (60¢) is fresh and syrupy sweet, and the Turkish coffee makes a fittingly rich accompaniment.

Note: There is another, newer, slightly higher priced Casbah at 3341 W. Dempster in Skokie.

# Cape Cod Room

140 E. Walton (at Michigan Ave.)
in the Drake Hotel
Phone: 787-2200
Parking: Street, garages, or doorman
Full bar
Credit Cards: American Express
Coat and tie required

Daily, Noon—Midnight
Reservations necessary

For years the Cape Cod Room has enjoyed the reputation as Chicago's best seafood house, and despite several worthy challengers, we still feel it is the king of the sea. What's impressive is not just the staggering variety of fresh and salt-water fish and shellfish offered, but the number of ways in which each is prepared. For example, lobster comes as newburg, thermidor, parisienne, and mornay, in addition to steamed or boiled. The standard repertoire is further augmented by seasonal specials, such as soft shell crabs, mahi-mahi, and grouper.

As the menu is a la carte, you won't escape without a noticeable dent in your pocketbook (even rolls cost 25¢ per person.) However, the value is generally excellent.

Begin your meal with the Cape Cod's justifiably renowned Bookbinder soup (95¢), chunky with red snapper and further perked with a vial of sherry. There are also cherrystone or little neck clams ($1.95) and a tangy, fresh-tasting shrimp cocktail ($2.35).

From the stream of entrees, we especially like the delicate sole amandine ($4.95), tender sauteed Cape Cod scallops ($6.85), and either lobster or crab newburg ($7.50 or $6.50). We found the pompano en papillote (cooked in parchment, along with lobster, mushrooms and red wine, $6.25), beautifully served but too strong-tasting.

The accompanying salad or cole slaw is tasty, but we have been disappointed by the somewhat gummy, bland au gratin potatoes. There is also a selective and agreeably priced wine list.

The cozy, rustic New England Inn atmosphere is delightful. Although Cape Cod has long had a reputation for snobby service, the staff seems to have mellowed considerably in recent years.

# *The Creole House

3048 W. Diversey
Phone: 772-1230
Parking: Street
B.Y.O.
No credit cards

Tue.-Thur., 5:00 P.M.—9:30 P.M.
Fri.-Sat., 5:00 P.M.—10:30 P.M.
Closed Sunday, Monday
Reservations necessary on weekends

From the moment you ring the bell at the Creole House, you know that you're in for a pleasurable evening. Located in an old Victorian house, the setting captures the feeling of faded but genteel southern aristocracy. There's dark wood trim, ornate Victorian spindlework, gold tie-back curtains, and subdued lighting. Service is most gracious.

The menu, offering complete dinners priced from $5.50 to $7.50, features several Creole specialties. The food, a combination of French, Spanish, African, and American Indian influences, is exotic and somewhat spicy, though not at all difficult to handle.

Meals begin with a simple but tasty shrimp paté. Soup is next, either a creamy peanut soup, a thick gumbo brimming with seafood, or a superb Bayou chili. Forego the salad, and try the tangy seven vegetable cole slaw. It is soon followed by a basket of hot, buttery French bread. Somewhere in between, we recommend ordering the wonderfully light, crisp corn fritters (70¢ extra), served with a small pitcher of honey.

Entrees feature three different Jambalayas—shrimp, chicken, or a Creole House special which includes a combination of chicken, ham, and a mildly spiced sausage ($6.75). They are served casserole style, mixed with rice and vegetables and topped with melted cheddar cheese. Other possibilities are Creole beef rolls ($7.50), southern fried chicken and corn fritters ($6.00), or tender Cajun catfish served with hushpuppies ($6.00).

Desserts are handwritten on a separate menu, and each is tempting. Try either the rich fudge-mint ice cream pie, sour cream pecan pie, or apple pecan pie and accompany it with a cup of chicory coffee.

# L'escargot

2929 N. Halsted
Phone: 525-5525
Parking: Street
Full bar
Credit Cards: Bank of America, Master Charge

Lunch: Mon.-Sat., 11:30 A.M. —2:00 P.M.
Dinner: Sun.-Thur., 5:00 P.M. —10:00 P.M.
Fri.-Sat., 5.00 P.M.—11:00 P.M.
Reservations necessary

Pastel-stained walls, baskets of fresh fruit at each setting, and a display table of mouth-watering desserts give L'escargot a charming, country ambience. The narrow bar, with its navy and white polka dot cloth-covered tables, offers limited but more intimate seating. Cooking is that of the French provinces, devotedly prepared. Complete dinners, often including a complimentary cold vegetable dish like ratatouille, range from $8.00 to $9.50.

For openers, try the celeri remoulade (grated celery root mixed with a tart mustardy mayonnaise sauce), the delicious but salty smoked filet of herring, or the superb sausage en croute (homemade sausage enclosed in the flakiest of crusts).

Soups, with the exception of the spritely watercress, are not particularly unusual. The simple, but perfectly-flavored salad which follows, is composed of tender Boston lettuce tossed with a tangy vinaigrette dressing.

The eight or so entrees vary, and among those we like best are the roast duck with either orange or cherry sauce and any of the fish. The fresh poached trout, stuffed with pureed mushrooms and topped by a light cream sauce, is particularly good. So are the coq au vin (which boasts a rich yet subtle sauce) and the beef stroganoff.

Among the fabulous desserts at L'escargot, the fruit tarte (especially strawberry-apricot) is perfection itself—a blend of flaky pastry, plump fruit, and delicate custard. There is an ample wine list too, and the $5 house version is quite good. Service is generally excellent (though, like anywhere, you can hit upon an off-night).

# *La Fontaine

2442 N. Clark
Phone: 525-1800
Parking: Free, in garage across street.
Full bar
Credit Cards: Bank of America, Master Charge
Jackets are preferred for men

Mon.-Sat., 5:30 P.M.—10:30 P.M.
Lunch, Tue.-Fri., 11:30 A.M. —2:30 P.M.
Reservations necessary

Both the cooking and the setting are exquisite at La Fontaine, one of Chicago's newer French restaurants, located in an attractively refurbished brownstone.

The $10.75 prix fixe dinner begins with a flourish, as the appetizers are pure pleasure. Highly recommended are la coquille Deauvilloise (hot seafood and mushrooms in a creamy champagne sauce) or le delice de La Fontaine (a blend of ham, fresh mushrooms, and melted cheese served over a toasted crouton). Also excellent are the light puffy quiche lorraine or the smooth salmon mousse with a green mayonnaise sauce.

Each of the three soups—the cheesy onion, St. Germain (pea soup with croutons,) and vichyssoise—is deftly prepared and subtly flavored. Good French bread and unsalted butter make a fine accompaniment. However, we found the Boston lettuce salad slightly watery and lacking flavor.

This disappointment is soon forgotten when the entrees appear. The crisp duck, thickly glazed with orange sauce and peaches, is a marvel (served for two). There are three inventive fish selections: trout soufflé with champagne sauce, sea bass flamed in pernod (served for two), and poached turbot with hollandaise. Filet mignon with Bearnaise sauce and sirloin sauteed with shallots are excellent, but the thin sliced veal sauteed with mushrooms, applejack, and cream sauce is served in a rather small portion. Marvelous soufflé potatoes and creamed spinach or a fresh vegetable with hollandaise sauce go along beautifully.

Desserts, though not spectacular, include a rich chocolate mousse and a splendid cream caramel. The wine list is fairly extensive and can be expensive.

# Gene and Georgetti's

500 N. Franklin
Phone: 527-3718
337-9560
Parking: Lot
Full bar
Credit Cards: American Express

Daily, 11:30 A.M.-12:30 A.M.
Closed Sunday
Reservations necessary

Gene and Georgetti's is an unpretentious steak house but we doubt you'll find a more gorgeous piece of beef in Chicago. They range in price from a good-sized "small" sirloin for $6.75 up to $9.95 for an enormous T-bone. The meat is of excellent quality, charred to perfection on the outside and tender and juicy inside.

If you prefer your meat embellished, give the pepper steak a try—big chunks of butter-tender sirloin are cooked in a savory wine sauce along with green peppers, onions, and mushrooms. Lamb chops ($6.95) are large and thick, and the liver ($5.75) is good too, although it is thick sliced rather than thin. The menu also sports several less expensive pasta dishes.

All entrees include a platter of crisp cottage fries and either a salad or cole slaw. The slaw is fresh tasting, though heavy on scallions, but the salad is nothing special.

If possible, reserve a table in the main first floor dining room (the restaurant has several rooms on two floors). Although somewhat noisy, this location offers the most attractive setting, less surly waiters, and an excellent spot to absorb the action. Gene and Georgetti's has always enjoyed a popular following among businessmen, both legitimate and otherwise, and it's fun to watch and listen to the wheeling and dealing. However, if nothing's shaking, the steaks will more than hold your attention.

*ITALIAN (SICILIAN)*

# Mama Lena's Italian Kitchen

24 E. Chicago
Phone: 337-4050
Parking: Street or pay lot next door
B.Y.O.
No Credit Cards

Daily, Seating at 6:00 P.M. and 8:30 P.M. only
Closed Sunday
Reservations necessary

Mama Lena's is more like an Italian home than a restaurant. There's no menu to order from. Instead, guests are treated to whatever Sicilian speciality Mama's been cooking in her kitchen. Dinners are served twice nightly, and the complete five course meal costs $6.90 per person.

Mama Lena seems to lavish the same kind of love and care on her patrons as she did in cooking for her family of nine children. She is ably assisted by two of the nine, Sal and Carl, who are raucous, good humored, and always ready to trade quips with the customers. One evening when we had requested water, they obliged with a length of hose hooked up from the kitchen. Sound crazy? It is, but, before the evening's over, a good-natured, familial camaraderie exists between proprietors and patrons.

The food doesn't take second billing as it's generally quite delicious. Mama Lena has a repertoire of thirty-six meals, among them linguine with clam sauce, canneloni, braccioli, and several veal and chicken dishes.

Each dinner begins with a good-sized antipasto salad—crisp greens, cherry tomatoes, Italian olives, provolone, salami—all sprinkled with a slightly salty oil and vinegar dressing. It is served with some heavenly oregano-spiced tomato bread. A pasta dish follows, perhaps a large plateful of fafalli (bow-noodles) topped by a delicate sauce concocted from fresh tomatoes, ricotta, and romano cheese, peas and onions. Very light and exquisite. Next comes the main course. On a recent visit we were treated to a ground sirloin-eggplant melange which also featured fresh mushrooms, tomatoes, and mozzarella. Dessert (somewhat ordinary cannoli) and excellent coffee round out the meal.

After dinner, Uncle Chico, a beautiful 89-year old with full beard and beret entertains with Italian street songs and conversation. The atmosphere is leisurely, informal, and friendly.

# El Piqueo

5427 N. Clark
Phone: 769-0455
Parking: Street
B.Y.O. (25¢ charge for glassware)
Credit Cards: American Express, Carte Blanche, Diners Club

Mon.-Sat., 5:00 P.M.—10:30 P.M.
Closed Sunday

While Piqueo may not be the most well known of our "splurges", a surprising number of people consider it their favorite Chicago restaurant. The distinctive Peruvian cuisine is delicious and shows obvious signs of painstaking care. Moises Asturrizaga serves as host while his sister, Juana, devotes her talent to the food. There is no written menu. Each night they serve a special five-course dinner at a fixed price that has recently gone up to $8.00.

A typical evening's meal might begin with escaveche, bite-sized pieces of raw turbot marinated in lemon and lime juice spiced with onions and a touch of cayenne. It's delicate, spicy and refreshing. For the next course you might luck upon copa, a divine blend of shrimp and broccoli in a spicy egg-based cream sauce. Soup's next and ranges from a gentle beef noodle to a hearty shrimp-vegetable.

Beef, prepared one of several ways, is generally the evening's entree. It might come grilled on a skewer, as a beautifully flavored stew or as filete en cebolla (beef sauteed with onions). If you call in a day in advance, Juana will prepare her specialty, duck a la pericuoli ($9.50). We've never put in the call yet, but hear its fantastic. Papas huancaina, boiled potatoes in a piquant cheese sauce are an excellent accompaniment to the meat.

A demitasse of coffee and a light, creamy flan close the meal. Service is as unobtrusive and smooth as the flan. Señor Asturrizaga usually wends his way among the tables in order to explain various dishes or just to converse.

The decor at Piqueo is as unique as the cuisine—lush llama rugs and colorful native weaving decorate the walls. Lighting is subdued, seating is comfortable, and an intimate, relaxing atmosphere prevails.

# *Peking Duckling House

2045 W. Howard
Phone: 338-2016
Parking: Street
Full bar
Credit Cards: American Express

Tue.-Thur., 11:00 A.M.—10:00 P.M.
Fri., 11:00 A.M.—Midnight
Sat., 5:00 P.M.—Midnight
Sun., 5:00 P.M.—10:00 P.M.

For anyone who hasn't tried Mandarin cooking, the Peking Duckling House is an excellent place to start. We feel that it consistently offers the city's best Northern Chinese cuisine, one that is characterized by a spicy yet subtle flavor and complex preparation. The extensive eight-page menu alone takes at least ten minutes to savor.

A complete dinner of soup, appetizer, main dish, rice, dessert, and tea costs at least $6.00 per person, as everything is priced a la carte. You can definitely eat more cheaply by foregoing one of the courses, though we don't suggest it.

We recommend opening your assault with either the sizzling rice soup (in which hot crisp rice cakes are ladled into a broth rich with black mushrooms, bamboo shoots, peppers, and carrots, $1.75 for two) or the thick, unusually flavored sour and hot soup ($1.75 for two). For an appetizer, we like the light crisp green onion cakes ($1.60, serves two or three) that practically disintegrate at first bite.

Outstanding among the entrees are Moo-shu pork ($4.25), a shredded meat, vegetable, and egg combination that you eat wrapped in thin pancakes, or the spicy Szechuan beef ($4.25), crunchy with bamboo shoots, celery, and green pepper. Two excellent dishes with a slight bite are chicken or shrimp with peanuts ($3.85 and $4.25). A mild alternative is chicken and vegetables served on a crisp bed of sizzling rice ($3.85). Duck should not be ignored, particularly the deep fried tea smoked duck ($5.90), served with steamed buns and plum sauce, or the pressed duck ($4.95).

For dessert, be sure to try apple or banana fritters ($1.40 for two). They're not the hard candy-coated version found in most Mandarin restaurants, but have a light puffy batter. They're flamed in a brandy-honey sauce, and help finish your evening with a flourish.

# Seven Hills East

3001 W. Peterson
Phone: 728-3600
743-4362
Parking: Street
Full bar
Credit cards: American Express, Carte Blanche

Mon.-Sat., 4:00 P.M.—1:00 A.M.
Sun., 2:00 P.M.—Midnight

The decor at Seven Hills is ornate and glittery, but don't let the sparkles blind you to some really good food. Once you bite into the crusty, buttery, homemade herb rolls, you realize that there are elaborate things going on in the kitchen too. Complete dinners, which feature a tasty minestrone, salad, entree, vegetable, potato, dessert, and coffee average around $6.00 ($4.50 for pasta).

The menu is exclusively Italian, leaning heavily toward northern specialties. The variety offered is extensive—thirteen veal dishes, seven chicken, and thirteen fish and shellfish, not to mention innumerable pastas. Some meals we've particularly enjoyed are medallions of veals with asparagus parmigiana ($6.00), veal piccanti (thin-sliced veal and lemon slivers lightly turned in a butter sauce, $5.50), veal scallopini with mushrooms and wine ($5.75), red snapper Francese (sauteed in lemon-butter, $5.50), and shrimp broiled with olive oil and lemon ($6.25). Chicken dishes are excellent, particularly the Vesuvio (sauteed with herbs, garlic, and potatoes, $5.75) and the crisp parmigiana ($5.50).

They also serve any kind of pasta you might desire from homemade ravioli ($4.75) to canelloni ($5.00) to rigatoni ($4.50). One of the best is homemade fettucini Alfredo, tossed with sweet butter and parmesan cheese ($4.50).

Dessert is luxurious. The rum-flavored spumoni is richer-tasting than usual. And as if it weren't enough, a three-tiered silver platter of fresh fruit and Italian cookies comes with it.

Service is concerned but not rushed, making Seven Hills a fine place for engaging in a leisurely eating extravaganza.

# Lunches

# The Dominion Room

501 Davis, Evanston
Phone: 328-5252
Parking: Street
Full bar

Lunch, Daily until 2:30 P.M.
Sunday dinner, 11:30 A.M.—7:30 P.M.

The Dominion Room is a refined, respectable-looking tea-room, (though liquor is now served). The food is wholesome American at its best, with homemade bread and desserts being the star attractions. Lunches average $2.50 (less for sandwiches), and the selection changes each day.

Starting on the light side, there is at least one special luncheon salad, perhaps Caesar (featuring great, sauteed croutons), mixed fruit, or a tomato stuffed with tuna salad. Salad dressings, especially the tarragon, are unusually tasty as they are made (and sold) on the premises. Sandwiches (averaging about $1.30) might include chicken salad on cracked wheat bread, ham and cheese, or corned beef.

If you'd prefer something hot, there are five to six entrees all of which come with either soup, salad or juice, rolls or bread, and vegetable. Some standouts are the moist, homey-tasting baked chicken ($2.50), broiled trout ($2.50), lamb stew in dill sauce ($2.50), and ham-broccoli casserole ($2.45). But just about everything's good. Unlike most restaurants, care is taken with vegetables. You might come upon "seven minute" cabbage, garden vegetable soufflé, mashed hubbard squash, or even rutabaga.

If you can fit in dessert and an extra 45¢, you won't be sorry. Live a little and try one of these: cherry or peach lattice pie a la mode, lemon meringue tart, applesauce cake with penuche frosting, or a meringue with ice cream and hot fudge sauce.

Complete dinners, including appetizer and dessert, are served every evening, with at least five choices being under our $4.50 budget.

# Epicurean

316 S. Wabash — Mon.-Fri., 11:00 A.M.—10:00 P.M.
Phone: 939-2190 — Sat., 11:00 A.M.—Midnight
Parking: Take the bus
Full bar

If you have to eat lunch downtown, you're generally better off bringing your own. Bright spots, budget-food wise, are few and far between. However, skip the salami sandwich one day, and try the Epicurean. It offers fine Hungarian cooking at reasonable prices and has long enjoyed a reputation for its homemade strudel.

Entrees are generally priced from $2.00 to $2.25. Some traditional favorites include Szekely goulash with noodles ($2.25), chicken paprikash ($2.25), Hungarian stuffed cabbage ($2.15), and Hungarian stuffed peppers ($2.15). If you're into something sweet, there's a fantastic apple-strawberry pancake ($2.00) as well as the special light Hungarian crêpe, palascinta ($2.00), filled with either cheese or jelly.

All entrees come with a small dish of pickled, whole baby beets and a basket of rolls. Complete luncheons, which include a bowl of homemade soup, beverage, and strudel—either apple or cheese—will cost you 85¢ to $1.00 more (a really good buy since the strudel alone is 75¢ a serving.) The strudel rightly deserves its fame; the leaves are paper thin and flaky, and the filling is fresh, abundant, and not overly sweet. It is served warm, dusted with powdered sugar.

The Epicurean is run as a good downtown restaurant should be. Service is prompt and efficient, but not unduly rushed. It's definitely a pleasant place to unwind.

Dinners here are higher priced, and include a complete meal. One compensation is that the best strudel of them all—cherry—is served only at night.

# F & T Restaurant

1182 N. Milwaukee — Daily, 5:30 A.M.—7:00 P.M.
Phone: 252-1150
Parking: Street
Full bar

A step inside the F & T takes you back in time. It has been a popular landmark in the old Polish neighborhood at Milwaukee and Division for fifty years. The restaurant still retains its old world atmosphere, with dark paneling, ornate ceiling, comfortable booths, and a scattering of bentwood coat racks. The food is prepared with old-fashioned care, even though it is served cafeteria style. Practically everything is made from scratch, including the baked beans, mayonnaise, and chocolate sauce.

Main courses can include just about anything. All are priced between $1.50 and $2.25, which includes two side dishes. There might be stuffed cabbage, roast chicken, Polish sausage, meat loaf, oxtail stew, chop suey, spare ribs, duck (Saturdays only), and baked steak smothered with vegetables (Sundays only). The stuffed cabbage and the sausage dishes are always tasty, but we don't particularly care for the meat loaf which is heavy with filler. Marinated cucumbers and a nice, tangy coleslaw are standout side dishes. Most of the cooked vegetables are best ignored.

A host of sandwiches are here for the carving, including corned beef, roast beef, ham, and perhaps turkey, all priced between $1.25 and $1.35 and served on fresh Rosen's rye. Soups (40¢) are homemade and filling, and the day's offering might include barley, lima bean, vegetable, mushroom, or beet.

If you can handle dessert, try either a prune or cheese blintz (45¢) hot off the griddle, or else go for the chocolate sundae (45¢).

F & T offers a feast of faces as well as food, as the place is frequented by a medley of Chicago characters.

# Magic Pan

60. E. Walton
Phone: 943-2456
Old Orchard Shopping Center
Phone: 677-2110
Parking: Walton (street)
Old Orchard (parking lot)
Full bar

Mon.-Fri., 11:00 A.M.—Midnight
Sat., 11:00 A.M.—2:00 A.M.
Sun., 11:00 A.M.—9:00 P.M.

Magic Pans are sunny, cheerfully-decorated restaurants that serve a tantalizing variety of crêpes. Lunches are a good bet price-wise, as a crêpe and salad duo costs under $3.00, while dinners generally run over $4.00. The scrumptious dessert crêpes are extra.

Some of our favorite choices are the light spinach soufflé crêpe or the curried chicken with a coconut-spiced apple topping. The ham and cheese combination consists of two crisp deep-fried crêpes, one filled with thin-sliced ham and the other with a sizzling melted cheese. Portions are deceivingly more filling than they look, though one can easily make room for dessert.

The crêpe a la mode ($1.75) is an indecently rich concoction, an ice cream-filled crêpe topped by a dark chocolate sauce. There's an apple crêpe ($1.45), a banana crêpe garnished with brown sugar sauce, whipped cream, and almonds ($1.65), and a cherries jubilee crêpe ($1.75). For an all-out splurge, order the Beignets—bow-shaped, deep-fried crêpes that are incredibly crisp and light. They are sprinkled with cinnamon and powdered sugar, and come with a dip of either brandied chocolate or apricot sauce. At $2.95, they're expensive, but the portion is immense, and if there was ever a time for being free with the bills, this is it.

Dining at the Magic Pan is a visual as well as a taste treat. There are several nice touches: fresh flowers on the table, hanging plants, sugar cubes in little wire baskets, and an abundance of fresh, spring colors.

Recently new Magic Pans have opened in the Woodfield Shopping Center and the Oakbrook Mall.

# Mallers Building Coffee Shop

5 S. Wabash, 3rd Floor
Phone: 263-7696
Parking: Take the "el"
No liquor

Mon.-Fri., 5:30 or 6:00 A.M.—5:00 P.M.
Sat., 7 A.M.—2:30 P.M.
Closed Sunday

Mallers is Chicago's hidden deli, located on the third floor of that famous downtown landmark, the Mallers Building. It's one of the Loop's best lunch spots and even boasts a picturesque view of the Wabash "el." A crowd gathers here at noon, and the scene is sometimes nothing short of frantic. The cooks are yelling in the kitchen, secretaries line up for carry-outs, and everyone else sits contentedly munching on chopped liver or corned beef omelettes.

The menu features most delicatessen standards. The corned beef sandwich ($1.45) is moist and flavorful, served in an adequate though not overpowering portion. The coarsely chopped liver has a nice texture and taste. There's a good combination plate for $1.90 that offers chopped liver, a cheese blintz, farmer's chop suey (fresh salad vegetables and sour cream), and fruit salad (which turns out to be canned fruit cocktail). The blintzes are delicious—delicate and crisp, with a sweet, mild cheese filling. There's also a lox and cream cheese plate, as well as an appealing chopped liver and potato pancake duo ($2.10).

Chocolate phosphates are good. So's the rye bread. The waitresses are true pros, so the service is short-order swift. It's a fun place to eat and sure beats Toffenetti's.

# *Manny's

1139 S. Jefferson
(off Roosevelt Road)
Phone: 939-2855
Parking: Rear lot and street
No liquor

Daily, 5:00 A.M.—5:30 P.M.
Closed Sunday

You'd almost think they were giving food away at Manny's, the way the crowd gathers at noon. You'll never see a broader cross-section of people eating in one restaurant. There are Roosevelt Road merchants, firemen from the nearby academy, hardhats, students, shoppers, etc., all converging on Manny's for the same reason: speedy service, low prices, and the most appealing and varied cafeteria-style food in the city.

There are about a dozen hot dishes offered daily at an inflation-fighting average of $2.00. Roast veal breast ($2.00), brisket ($2.20), short ribs ($2.15), chicken pot pie ($1.80), spaghetti and meatballs ($1.95), gefilte fish ($1.90), oxtail stew ($1.95), corned beef and cabbage ($2.20), and prune tzimmes ($2.15) are just a sampling. They all are tasty and served in truck-driver portions. Potato and vegetable are included.

Manny's makes a great-looking, great-tasting corned beef sandwich, served on rye or an onion roll. There's also brisket, tongue, ham, pastrami, and roast beef. All cost $1.40 and are served with a potato pancake and kosher pickle.

The side dishes are terrific, with the Jewish big "K's" being well represented. There's kishke, knish, kreplach and kasha (the latter two come in chicken soup). Each costs 45¢, and the meat-filled knish is particularly delish.

Desserts are almost as varied as the entrees. Priced from 20¢ to 50¢, there are cream pies, rice pudding, cherry squares, canned figs, sugarless baked apples, and Napoleons.

# *San Pedro

In Plaza del Lago
Shopping Center
(just off Sheridan
Road, in Wilmette)
Phone: 251-6621
Parking: Lot
B.Y.O.

Tue.-Sat., 11:30 A.M.—2:30 P.M.
Sun., 12:15 A.M.—8.00 P.M.
Closed Monday

San Pedro is a blissful place for lunch. Despite its name, only the architecture and handsome decor are Spanish. The food is strictly American tearoom with a slight French accent.

Just one glance at the menu is a Pavlovian experience. It's one of the most mouthwatering we've ever read. There's an omelette with fresh strawberries and sour cream ($2.35), quiche lorraine ($2.50), and cheddar cheese soufflé ($2.95). Our special favorite is mushrooms polonaise ($2.50), a flaky pastry shell filled with fresh mushrooms in a delicate sour cream-flavored sauce. An unusual and appealing dish is the pecan loaf with mushroom sauce ($2.35). It tastes something like bread dressing for turkey, and is really quite delicious. Don't overlook the more mundane but excellent roast beef hash, topped by a poached egg and velvety tomato sauce ($2.35). A variety of luncheon salads and sandwiches is available too.

Most lunches include a small salad (the white asparagus-pineapple-watercress combination is exquisite), a good and gooey homemade caramel roll and either soup or dessert. However, if you are able to resist the alluring desserts—fudge pie a la mode, rhubarb-strawberry pie, banana cream pie—you deserve a citation from Dr. Stillman.

Expect a wait at San Pedro. The restaurant rivals backgammon in popularity among the suburban set.

San Pedro serves excellent dinners for an average of $5.00. Dinner hours are: Tues.-Fri., 5:15 P.M.—8:00 P.M.; Sat., 5:15 P.M.—9:00 P.M.; Sun., 12:15 A.M.—8:00 P.M.

# Tel Aviv

6349 N. California
Phone: 764-3776
Parking: Street
No liquor

Daily, 11:30 A.M.—9:00 P.M.
Closed Friday sundown to Saturday sundown

Step inside the Tel Aviv, and it's as if you are no longer in Chicago. Hebrew is the prevailing language, men and boys wear yalmulkes, and Israeli flags and posters decorate the walls. Tel Aviv is a dairy restaurant (no meat is served) and primarily offers middle-eastern specialties: falafel (deep-fried balls of ground chick peas and spices), chomos (a ground chick pea spread), and chopped eggplant salad. There are also a few typical Jewish deli offerings—gefilte fish, lox, and beet borscht. And would you believe kosher pizza?

Food is serve-yourself, with several dishes displayed on a steam table. The falafel (45¢ or 80¢) is superb here. It's crisp, dripping with salad and sauce and practically overflows its pocketed middle eastern bread. Baked fish ($2.50), smothered in a celery-mushroom-studded tomato sauce, is another possible luncheon choice. We also like their cheese-filled french fried cauliflower (60¢ a serving). Remember to sample the pizza. It's 50¢ a slice, very garlicky and not bad at all!

# Brunches

## Casa Bonnifeather

2449 N. Lincoln
Phone: 929-2570
Parking: Street
B.Y.O.

Sunday Brunch: Noon—3:00 P.M.

A quiet, genteel setting for brunch. The lighting is subdued, the music classical and the waiters attentive. The meal begins with a continental touch—a basket of long thin French bread and fresh fruit. Entrees include four appealing egg dishes, several gruyere-based quiche lorraines, and French toast with rolled ham. Among our favorites are the frittata, an Italian inspired omelette studded with fresh mushrooms, ham, mozzarella cheese and herbs ($2.50), and either vegetarian (primarily onion and zucchini) or herbed tomato quiche ($2.50). Juice (orange or V-8) and coffee or tea are included.

Casa Bonnifeather also serves unusual, primarily cheese-based dishes for dinner, in the $4.40 to $5.25 range.

## The Court House

5211 S. Harper
(in Harper Court
shopping mall)
Phone: 667-4008
Parking: Street
Full bar

Sunday Brunch: 11:00 A.M.—3:00 P.M.

This is the place to come if you wake up starving on a Sunday morning. The Court House presents an all-you-can-eat buffet of truly stomach-stretching proportions. There's something here to please everyone, ranging from squeeze-your-own orange juice to french fried clams. In between you'll find breakfast, lunch, and dinner all in one: fresh fruit, scrambled eggs, deviled eggs, quiche lorraine, cheeses, cold cuts, smoked fish, lox (sometimes), hashed brown potatoes, chopped liver, fried chicken, mostaciolli, tossed salad, jello mold, three-bean salad, and a mountain of kaiser rolls, bagels, and raisin bread. Also some delicious coffee.

Prices have escalated to a rather steep $4.50 (kids, $2.25), but it's still one of the best bets in restaurant-hungry Hyde Park. Always crowded but airy and spacious in feel.

# Evanston Inn

840 Forest, Evanston Sunday meal: 1:00 P.M.—7:00 P.M.
Phone: 864-5000
Parking: Street
No liquor

For those who might be in the mood for an early Sunday dinner rather than a brunch, the Evanston Inn offers a classic buffet in the church social tradition. There are jello molds, salads galore (potato, macaroni, carrot and raisin, three bean, mixed fruit, tossed greens, cole slaw) and a mound of homemade rolls. Among the hot offerings you might find stuffed pork chops, roast beef, biscuit-topped creamed chicken, mashed potatoes, stewed tomatoes, carrots, and creamed turnips. Be sure to save some room for the homemade desserts, perhaps rhubarb pie, coconut custard pie, lemon meringue pie, and German chocolate cake. A few might be lopsided or look like rejects at a state fair, but all are tasty and cooked with love by the amiable chef.

The atmosphere at Evanston Inn is almost more intriguing than the food. It is obviously a place with a past and has aged noticeably but graciously. Ornately carved antiques are everywhere. The dining room itself features impressive stained glass, gold wallpaper, and an antique couch perched right in the center of everything. The whole place is imbued with a lovely aura of fading gentility that would comfort Tennessee Williams.

All this for $4.00.

# Lee's Canton Cafe

2300 S. Wentworth
Phone: 225-4838
Parking: Street
B.Y.O.

Sunday dim sum brunch:
11:00 A.M.—2:00 P.M.

On Sundays, Chinese and non-Chinese families alike gather at Lee's for a Sunday brunch unlike any other. It features at least thirteen different varieties of dim sum. What are they?—an unusual array of steamed or fried dumplings and pastries filled with meat, fish, vegetables, or sweets. Most are dainty, snack-like morsels, costing about 60¢ for two to three pieces.

You have to get here early to try the egg puff, a sweet melt-in-your-mouth, sugar sprinkled cruller. They're delicate and delicious, and so popular that Lee's is liable to run out. If so, don't despair. There are other goodies, including a large pork-filled bun called cha shu bow; woo gok, crisp deep-fried meat-filled potatoes, and sui mi, steamed won ton-like dough filled with chopped meat. There's also a tasty deep-fried bean cake containing egg, green, onion, and minced meat.

Unlike New York where they pass the dim-sum tray around so that customers can point and pick, at Lee's you'll have to take a chance. Ask your waiter for advice, and, after a few meals, you'll become a pro.

Lee's is good for other occasions, too, and makes delicious noodle soups and fantastic fried rice.

## Mr. Ricky's

9300 N. Skokie,
Skokie
Phone: 674-9300
Parking: Lot
No liquor

Sunday brunch, 10:00 A.M.—2:00 P.M.

Mr. Ricky's undoubtedly has the best brunch deal in town, especially if your idea of paradise is an unlimited supply of lox. For $3.25 (kids under 6, $1.95), you can feast on a buffet of lox (both Nova and salted), two other kinds of smoked fish, pickled herring, cream cheese, four types of bagels (rye, plain, onion, and poppyseed), kaiser and onion rolls, tomatoes, cucumbers, onions, noodle pudding, and deliciously sweet fried smelts. There's also orange juice, your choice of either fried or scrambled eggs (cooked to order), and doughnuts or sweet rolls.

## *The Original Pancake House

153 Greenbay Road,
Wilmette
Phone: 251-6003
1517 E. Hyde Park,
Chicago
Phone: 288-2322
Parking: Lot or street
No liquor

Daily (including Sunday),
7:00 A.M. 10:00 P.M.
Fri., 7:00 A.M.—11:00 P.M.
Sat., 7:00 A.M.—1:00 A.M.
Also, 202 N. Lincoln Pk.
10437 S. Western
621 E. St. Charles Rd.

The ultimate of pancake houses! The most voluptuous offering is the apple pancake, an incredibly rich, puffy, baked pancake filled with fresh sauteed apples and topped by a cinnamon-caramel glaze. (The regular size at $1.50 is enough for one person.) If you're not up to the apple, there's a more delicate baked German pancake sprinkled with powdered sugar and served with fresh lemon wedges ($1.25).

The rolled crêpes—mandarin orange ($1.50), cherry kijafa ($1.50), lingonberry ($1.50), and strawberry ($1.50)—are great. And if you're in the mood for something less flamboyant, there are buttermilk (90¢) and wheat germ pancakes ($1.20), plus a good plain waffle ($1.00). Great coffee!

# Vittles

2942 N. Clark  Sunday brunch: 11:30 A.M.—4:00 P.M.
Phone: 549-2060
Parking: Street
Full bar

In an attractive setting replete with hanging plants and a scattering of antiques, Vittles is one of our favorite places for brunch. The menu offers several beguiling selections. Heading the list is deftly-prepared eggs benedict, served on buttery English muffins with a delicious hollandaise, thick slices of ham, and a sprinkling of capers ($3.50). Its close rival, eggs Florentine, is a bubbly hot blend of baked eggs, spinach, and cream sauce ($3.50). The omelettes are imaginative, ranging from a shrimp and crabmeat duo ($3.95) to one filled with sweet apricot halves and sour cream ($3.95). All egg dishes are served with hash browns, toast, and a garnish of fresh fruit.

The mood is relaxed and unrushed (though you may have a wait to be seated.) Altogether a fine place for a Sunday morning.

## More Brunch and Breakfast Ideas:

The previously mentioned $3.95 buffet at Martingayle's, and the Bagel's amazing scrambled omelettes. Also R. J. Grunt's really outdoes itself with its $3.50 brunch-buffet.

Burt's Coffee Shop at 2800 W. Foster makes good lox and onion omelettes ($2.10), fried matzoh ($1.65), and marvelously crusty French toast made from thick sliced challe ($1.45). The Victoria Restaurant, a raunchy diner just west of the Belmont "el" (953 W. Belmont) dishes up some delicious buttery, vanilla-flavored French toast for 75¢. The pancakes at Steak n' Eggers (2100 N. Clark, 2737 N. Clark, 1174 W. Cermak, 1106 W. 95th) are generally reliable, and the Unique Delicatessan at 1501 E. 53rd in Hyde Park is a nice place for coffee and bagels. If you're really broke, the Hamburger King serves two eggs, hash browns, and toast for 45¢.

# Sandwiches

# Corned Beef

You can certainly find a decent corned beef sandwich in Chicago. With prices going up, you may not be able to afford one, but it's still comforting to know that they are out there. The following are among the best and, fortunately, are not too outrageously priced.

## *Braverman's

1604 W. Chicago
Phone: 421-3979

Daily, 10:00 A.M.—8:00 P.M.
Closed Sunday

Chicago's most popular place for corned beef. Why?—because they're huge. Your $1.85 buys a whopping mound of juicy, thin-sliced, good quality meat piled between two fresh slices of rye (or an onion roll or maybe, a kaiser roll). A crisp kosher dill is the lone companion.

Braverman's is primarily serve-yourself, which is fine because the skillful men who carve the meat are interesting to watch. They cut delicious brisket sandwiches ($1.85) too. And if you're strong of stomach, good kishke (30¢) and greasy potato pancakes (30¢) can be hard to resist.

Big stampede around noon. Cross-section crowd. A fun place.

## Jerry's Food and Liquors

215 E. Grand
Phone: 337-2500

Daily, 6:30 A.M.—6:30 P.M.
Sat., 6:30 A.M.—1:00 P.M.
Closed Sunday

A noisy workingman's sandwich shop where the name of the game is crunch the customer. If you're not ready to bark out your order when the counterman calls on you, watch out. Not for the timid or indecisive, at least during the noon crush. A better-than-average corned beef sandwich—lean, meaty, succulent ($1.50). Also good pastrami ($1.50) and boiled ham ($1.25).

Eating is done at counters. Carry outs available. Much calmer during off hours, but you miss some of the atmosphere.

## Purple Pickle

3463½ N. Broadway
Phone: 549-7577

Daily, 8:00 A.M.—11:00 P.M.
Sat.-Sun., 8:00 A.M.—10:30 P.M.

There's not only plain corned beef ($1.70) but triple deckers with swiss cheese, cole slaw, and thousand island dressing (be sure to ask for rye toast or you may get white, $2.10), hot corned beef and chopped liver combos ($2.10), and corned beef, lettuce, tomato, Russian dressing, and egg ($1.85). Good brisket sandwich ($1.85) and tasty soups, including a thick mushroom barley (65¢, 85¢).

Over six dozen sandwiches in all served up in this purple-walled place. Mort, of neighboring Mort's Home Catering, owns it.

## S & S Deli (Goldie's Pump Room)

594 Roger Williams,
Highland Park
Phone: 432-0775

Daily, 6:00 A.M.—8:00 P.M.
Saturday, 6:00 A.M.—7:30 P.M.
Sunday, 6:00 A.M.—7:00 P.M.

A little grocery-candy store cum deli run by Mildred and Aaron Goldstein. Terrific lean corned beef sandwiches—thick, fresh, and made by Goldie himself. Not only great-tasting but cheap ($1.35). Also more of the same with excellent roast beef ($1.35).

Goldie is a character, and his place has an old-time, personal feel. People come from near (and far).

Directions: Take Edens Expressway to Clavey Road turnoff, east to Greenbay. Turn north on Greenbay to Roger Williams and east a block or so.

# Gyros and Souvlaki

About a year and a half ago, gyros swept through Chicago faster than anything since the great fire. Just in case you've been out of town, gyros is a mixture of spicy lamb and beef pressed into a loaf and then broiled on a vertically spinning rotisserie. The browned meat is sliced thin, then piled onto pancake-sized grilled pita bread along with sliced tomatoes, onions, and perhaps parsley, oregano, paprika, and a yogurt-sour cream sauce.

How can you spot a good one? The meat should be crusty yet juicy, not too greasy, well-seasoned without being overpowering, and laid on thick. Pita is best grilled till golden and puffy and just brushed with oil, rather than bathed in it.

Don't overlook souvlaki (shish kabob), as either it or gyros makes a terrific $1.25 snack.

After a year of gyros, souvlaki, and Di-gel, here are our picks:

## Angie's

1971 N. Lincoln
Phone: 929-8300

Daily, 9:00 A.M.—1:00 A.M.
Closed Sunday

More spread out and diversified (fried chicken, pizza) than other gyroterias, Angie's still gets together a commendable gyros. It's juicy, crisp, and spicy with a tart lemon-garlic flavor. Moist yet well-cooked pita, yogurt sauce, and lots of tomatoes combine to make Angie's gyros a fine all-rounder. Cold, flaky, baklava (35¢) is excellent here.

## Athenian Room

807 W. Webster
Phone: 348-5155

Daily, 11:30 A.M.—11:30 P.M.

Gyros with a difference. The meat is more ground-beef textured than usual and red barbeque sauce (optional) is used in place of yogurt. Both take some getting used to, but once you do you may never switch. Terrific, very tender souvlaki. And great, thick Greek french fries, sprinkled with lemon juice and oregano.

This friendly, hang-loose place adjoins Glasgott's Groggery, and the twain often does meet. Also a few outdoor tables for sitting, weather and politicians permitting.

## Elihniko Souvlaki

2602½ W. Lawrence
Phone: 334-3855

Daily, 11:00 A.M.—11:00 P.M.

A tiny, funky, hole-in-the-wall in Greektown that serves great souvlaki (no gyros). Big, juicy chunks of lamb served on crisp, honey-colored pita. The whole thing's sprinkled with lemon juice, paprika, oregano, an optional yogurt-cucumber sauce, and, of course, tomatoes and onions. Very potent. Very authentic.

## Gyros King

3152 N. Broadway
Phone: 472-4300

Daily, 10:00 A.M.—2:00 A.M.

Big, heaping portion of well-seasoned gyros, lots of onions and tomatoes and nicely grilled, not too oily, pita. One complaint, the meat isn't always cut crisp enough. You used to have to request sour cream-yogurt sauce, but now they put it on automatically (so say something if you don't want it.) Gyros King is where we tried our first gyros, and it really flipped us. Though we no longer cartwheel, it's still a mighty good sandwich.

## Olympos Gyros

2665 N. Clark
Phone: 871-2810

Daily, 11:00 A.M.—Midnight
Fri.-Sat., 11:00 A.M.—1:00 A.M.

Lean, crisp but still juicy gyros. Served with ample onions and sauce, but skimpy with the tomatoes. Pita is well browned, but not greasy. Souvlaki doesn't fare as well. The lamb cubes are good-sized, but they're usually kind of tough. Fresh tasting, flaky baklava (45¢) prepared by owner's mother.

## *Samiramis

5253 N. Clark
Phone: 784-8616

Daily, 11:00 A.M.—11:00 P.M.
Fri.-Sat., 11:00 A.M.—2:00 A.M.

Tucked in between restaurants proffering limpa bread and Swedish meat balls, Samiramis remains strictly Greek. Not even a hint of cardamom in the gyros. And they do make a great one here. Well-packed, lots of meat, and nicely crusty (the cook is careful to let the meat brown.) Excellent lemon-flavored shish kabob (souvlaki). A gyros-shish kabob combo ($1.65) is also available. Marvelous, syrupy, cinnamon-flavored baklava (50¢).

## Sparta Gyros

3205 N. Broadway
Phone: 549-4210

Daily, 11:00 A.M.—2:00 A.M.

The most unassuming-looking of the Broadway gyros line-up. Not only do they make an excellent, potent, very meaty gyros, but one of the cooks is a treat to watch for his efficient (we should say, spartan) assembling of a sandwich. The souvlaki has a nice tangy flavor, but the sandwich could be heftier. A polished, spotless place.

# Hamburgers

We're a nation of hamburger eaters. Unfortunately many people have settled for a pre-packaged, anemic slab disguised with extras and served on a bleached-out bun that now passes for a hamburger. If you're looking for the real thing—all beef, thick, juicy, cooked to order and served on dark rye or maybe a good kaiser roll—do not despair. The following restaurants do the hamburger proper justice:

## Chicago Claim Company

2314 N. Clark
Phone: 871-1770

Tue.-Sun., 11:30 A.M.—Midnight
Fri.-Sat., 11:30 A.M.—1:00 A.M.
Closed Monday

The Claim Company does let you add garnishes to your hamburger, and good ones like sauteed mushrooms, french fried onions, swiss cheese, and teriyaki sauce. However, underneath it all, there's decent meat to be found. Our only question—why the pale, ungrilled bun?

Actually, once you've feasted on their lavish burger, crisp cottage fries, and excellent all-you-can-eat salad (fresh mushrooms, cherry tomatoes, etc.), you tend to forget about the bun. The whole thing costs $3.15, and we think you get your money's worth.

There's more to the menu than the hamburger, most of it priced beyond our reach. All is served in a setting cleverly and expensively designed around a gold mining theme.

One major drawback: The place is literally a gold mine and a wait for a table is inevitable (no reservations).

## Cooper and Cooper

4748 N. Kimball
Phone: 539-3968

Daily, 24 hours

Some night when you're in the mood for an old-time hamburger, sizzled while you watch and dripping with fried onions, head for Cooper and Cooper. Their meat is fresh ground (not pre-wrapped in patties), and the burger comes out properly juicy (a little greasy, maybe, but really juicy). The bun is grilled too, and the whole affair meshes perfectly. And it costs 60¢ (70¢ with cheese).

## Goldstein's

7308 Circle, Forest Park
(1 block west of Harlem;
1 block south of Lake St.)

Daily, 5:00 P.M.—1:00 A.M.
Closed Sunday

A local, timeless sort of lounge that serves a fantastic ½ lb. "Goldyburger." The striking thing about the burger is that it tastes so good. We don't quite know why, it just does. You can have your Goldyburger plain ($1.75) or fancy. Try the Hawaiian (topped with pineapple and crisp bacon, $2.25) or the Royal burger (with bacon and cheese, $2.25). Only the mushroom burger ($2.15) is a disappointment, as the mushrooms are neither sauteed nor fresh.

Standard french fries come with (don't bother with the potato pancakes,) and you can include a good, heaping tossed salad ($1.00). Service is friendly.

## *Hackney's

Harm's Road (south of Lake Avenue), Glenview
Phone: 724-5577
Lake Avenue (east of Waukegan Road), Glenview
Phone: 724-7171
Milwaukee Avenue (south of Dundee), Wheeling
Phone: 537-2100
Route 12 (1 mile north of Route 22), Lake Zurich
Phone: 438-2103

Daily, 11:30 A.M.—12:30 A.M.

For some people, the "only" hamburger. We remember when it was 95¢. Others can go further back. Now the Hackneyburger's up to $2.20 (and the size seems to be getting smaller.) Fortunately, quality and taste are still excellent. Perfectly cooked, super juicy, and served on fresh dark rye. And it's pure ambrosia when the coarse-grained rye soaks in the meat juices.

A platter of good french fries and a cup of tart, creamy cole slaw are included. But don't forget Hackney's french fried onions ($1.30)—they're another institution. Served in a loaf, they're thin-sliced, crisp, coated with the featheriest of batters, slightly greasy, and great. In fact, we've tasted none better. The best turkey sandwich in town, too. Always crowded.

## John Barleycorn Memorial Pub

658 W. Belden — Daily, 11:30 A.M.—1:00 A.M.
Phone: 348-8899

Still an old standby for good cheddarburgers ($2.05), roquefort burgers ($2.05), cheeseless burgers ($1.80), and chiliburgers ($2.05) on dark bread. John Barleycorn was one of the earliest places to serve cottage fries.

Mixed highbrow media—art slides, classical music, and silent movies. Dark, atmospheric, and just crowded enough.

## *MacDuff's

4035 W. Fullerton — Daily, 11:00 A.M.—9:00 P.M.
Phone: 235-0408

A friendly, boisterous local bar serving Chicago's true Big Mac—a gigantic beefburger ("hamburger" is a forbidden word) weighing in at over three-quarters of a pound. The lean, succulent burger costs $2.25 and is made from prime ground round. No extra trimmings, but it's served on your choice of black bread, rye, or an onion roll. Mediocre french fried onions, french fries, and a good dill pickle come along. Colorfully presided over by Ogden, Bookie and Billy MacDuff, a father-sons team, their beefburger tends to put others to shame, and they're mighty proud of it.

## Otto's

2024 N. Halsted
Phone: 528-2230

Daily, 4:00 P.M.—2:00 A.M.
Sat., 11:00 A.M.—3:00 A.M.
Sun., 11:00 A.M.—2:00 A.M.

Otto's makes a fine hamburger—chunky, moist, and filling. No special frills, but good quality meat and a chewy kaiser-type roll. It comes with fries and costs $1.85 ($1.95 with cheese).

There are tempting side dishes like corn on the cob (50¢), but don't be beguiled by the onion rings ($1.00), as they're disguised beneath breading. Otto's also makes good home-made soups ($1.00 for a big bowl) and chili with burgundy wine ($1.00).

Cozy pub atmosphere and pleasant summer beer garden. Mainly a young crowd.

## Sauer's

311 E. 23rd Street
Phone: 225-6171

Daily, 11:00 A.M.—9:00 P.M.
Closed Sunday

A fat, round, perfectly charred hamburger wedged between two slices of rye! Excellent taste. The $1.85 price includes french fries and slaw. Good, potent barbeque sauce served on the side. The menu also includes a fine roast beef sandwich ($1.55) and an inexpensive daily special like Tuesday's pot roast, red cabbage, and potato dumplings ($1.75).

Everything's done smoothly in this mammoth, reconverted warehouse. Very popular for lunch, and just a few blocks from McCormick Place.

## The Winery

2906 N. Mannheim,
Franklin Park
Phone: 455-4041

Daily, 11:00 A.M.—Midnight
Sat.-Sun., Noon—Midnight

This isn't the best of our hamburgers, but do they have a gimmick! With your burger, you get all the red wine you can drink plus a serve-yourself salad bar and fries. And the hamburger's really pretty good—thick and served on black bread. The whole thing goes for $3.50.

Directions: The Winery's hidden behind a drive-in called Dave's Hamburgers. Take either Eisenhower Expressway to Mannheim (turn north) or Kennedy Expressway to Mannheim (turn south).

* * *

# Hotdogs

Sorry, we had to draw the line somewhere. Though we know it's un-American, we just don't like hotdogs. We thought about having someone do our "research" for us, but . . .

Anyway, if we do get the urge, we head for a beach refreshment stand (the hotdog's nothing special, but what great brown mustard) or a pushcart vendor. Some true fans swear by Fluky's (6740 N. Western), Terry's (2721 W. Touhy), and Wolfy's (2734 W. Peterson). And we've got to admit that Chicago does make a superlative rendition—try getting one with celery salt and tomatoes in Oshkosh.

# Italian Beef

Italian beef stands are a Chicago institution. They rank right behind taverns, funeral parlors, and hot dog stands in number. Beef places can usually be recognized by their seediness, garishness, or both. However there are times when nothing tastes better than a juicy, dripping beef sandwich on soft French bread.

Beef stands offer three basics: plain beef sandwiches, Italian sausage sandwiches, and the real masterpiece, a beef and sausage combination, always referred to as a "combo". Also there is the option of adding sweet green peppers and/or a spoonful of hot pepper salad. The pepper salad can usually be found on the counter and is only for the iron-mouthed.

How can you recognize a superior sandwich? Look for juicy, paper-thin sliced beef piled with abandon atop fresh bread. It should become soggier as you eat until it almost collapses. A good one always requires at least three napkins. The best sausage is barbequed rather than steamed, so that the outside skin is crisp and the meat spicy and succulent.

The following are some of the most pure Chicago:

## *Al's Bar BQ

1075 W. Taylor

Daily, 10:00 A.M.—1:00 A.M.
Fri.-Sat., 10:00 A.M.—2:00 A.M.

Always crowded, open-air place (moves indoors in winter) across from Italian lemonade stand. Good, big, soggy, sandwich. Huge, crisp, charcoal-broiled sausage. Lively place, lots of action. Beautiful example of pre-Circle Campus Taylor Street atmosphere.

Beef or Sausage: 80¢
Combo: $1.10

## Carm's Bar-B-Q

804 S. Cicero
Phone: 287-3930

Daily, 8:00 A.M.—6:00 P.M.
Fri.-Sat., 8:00 A.M.—8:00 P.M.

Was for many years "the" beef stand—the one you traveled miles to get to at 11:00 on a Saturday night. Still a good sandwich. Not too spicy—lots of meat. Charcoaled sausage. Big, roomy, air conditioned. Classic beef stand atmosphere.

Beef or sausage sandwich: 90¢
Combo: $1.10

There is also Carm's #2 at 7101 W. Roosevelt in Berwyn.

## *Margie's Bar-B-Q

1324 N. Cicero
Phone: 378-9733

Daily, 10:30 A.M.—12:45 A.M.
Fri.-Sat., 10:30 A.M.—1:45 A.M.

One of the best beefs around. Very juicy—oodles of beef. Chewy bread—just soggy enough. Charcoaled sausage. Cramped, no seating indoors, but nice tree-shaded picnic tables outside.

Beef or Sausage: 80¢
Combo: $1.05

## Mr. Beef

666 N. Orleans
Phone: 337-8500

Daily, 8:00 A.M.—8:00 P.M.
Sat., 8:00 A.M.—3:00 P.M.

Best beef near the loop—swamped at lunch. Peppery beef. Bread soaks in juice nicely. Clean, shiny, stand-up counter. Also enclosed picnic tables outside with good view of factories and traffic.

Beef: 90¢
Sausage: 70¢
Combo: $1.10

## *Roma's

6161 N. Milwaukee
No phone

Daily, 11:00 A.M.—Midnight
Fri.-Sat., 11:00 A.M.—2:00 A.M.

Huge meat portions make this the biggest beef sandwich around. Also a generous slice of charcoal-broiled sausage. Moderately spicy. Excellent hot pepper salad, which is also for sale by the jar. Only beef stand with booths plus counter. Air-conditioned.

Beef or Sausage: 95¢
Combo: $1.25

## Top This

4365 N. Sheridan
Phone: 528-1343

Mon.-Thur., 10:00 A.M.—9:00 P.M.
Fri.-Sun., 10:00 A.M.—1:00 A.M.

There's good beef to be found among the fast foods of this Uptown all-purpose eatery. Spicy beef, juicy sandwich. Sausage tasty, but steamed rather than charcoaled. Long salmon-colored counter, brighter-than-life lights. Adjoins bowling alley.

Beef: 95¢
Sausage: 85¢
Combo: $1.25

# Submarines

Submarine sandwiches range from the great and bountiful to those that should remain permanently submerged.

Among the former:

## Capt'n Nemo's

7367 N. Clark
Phone: 973-0570

Daily, 11:00 A.M.—10:00 P.M.
Closed Sunday

A friendly, family-run operation. Everything's out on display, making it easy to select what looks good. The "Sea Farer's" our choice—scrumptious tuna salad, brick cheese, hard boiled egg, tomato and lettuce on French bread (two sizes: 90¢ and $1.70). Two other good ones: "Super cheese" with American, Swiss, brick, muenster and provolone ($1.20 and $2.30) and "Italian Swiss," mainly Italian hard salami and Swiss cheese ($1.10 and $2.10).

A different homemade soup each day and desserts, including eclairs and homemade cheesecake. Bright colors. Nautical look. A thoroughly nice place.

## George's Sub Station

1203 W. Bryn Mawr
Phone: 784-9151

Daily, 10:00 A.M.—Midnight
Fri.-Sat., 10:00 A.M.—1:00 A.M.

George bills itself as offering the "king of submarine sandwiches." While we wouldn't go that far, they do make a decent one. The main pluses: lots of meat, fresh bread, and herbs. Try the "little king sub" (ham, mortadella, salami, American cheese, and fine shredded lettuce, 70¢ and $1.30).

## Little King

6461 N. Sheridan
Phone: 761-2163

Mon.-Thur., 10:00 A.M.—1:00 A.M.
Fri.-Sat., 10:00 A.M.—2:00 A.M.
Sun., Noon—1:00 A.M.

A popular place for subs among the bright lights of the Loyola strip. Eleven different combinations. All have a healthy sprinkling of oil, vinegar, and oregano plus finely shredded lettuce, tomatoes, mayonnaise, and onions (optional). We like the #1—prosciutto, salami, and provolone ($1.11; $2.00). Most of the meat is sliced to order.

## Mario's

1635 W. Taylor
Phone: 226-8491

Daily, 8:00 A.M.—5:00 P.M.
Closed Sunday

An atmospheric place filled with dark booths, hanging coconut heads, pictures of the Blackhawks, and a 1931 newspaper headlining "Capone gets eleven years." Club-like feeling. Very Italian.

The food may take second place, but not by much. A great sub is the "Mario special," stuffed with ham, mortadella, salami, provolone, lettuce, and tomato ($1.85). Also, spicy meatball sandwiches (95¢ and $1.55), Italian sausage (95¢ and $1.55) and on Fridays, pepper and egg ($1.10 and $1.60).

## *Submarine Sandwich Shop

1324 W. Grand
Phone: 226-9648

Daily, 6:30 A.M.—5:00 P.M.
Sat., 8:00 A.M.—5:00 P.M.
Closed Sunday

Look for the painting of Popeye on the window to locate this fine sub stand. Fresh ingredients: lots of ham plus salami, swiss cheese, tomatoes, lettuce (shredded, but not the stringy kind), oregano, and oil. Excellent flavor, and prices are good too. Subs come in three sizes, priced at 90¢, $1.05, and $1.25. Run by a pleasant couple, their place also doubles as a small grocery store. A few tables. Brisk, fast-moving lunch business.

* * *

# Miscellaneous Sandwiches

## Bungalow Inn

2835 N. Racine
Phone: 281-9829

Daily, 11:30 A.M.—10:00 P.M.
Closed Sunday

A pine-panelled German bar specializing in sausages and neat open face sandwiches. Good, thin-sliced, rare roast beef on rye ($1.55). Sausage sandwiches are $1.10 or you can have a bratwurst, knackwurst or thueringer plate with sauerkraut and either a boiled potato or German potato salad ($1.75).

# *The Falafel King

4507 W. Oakton, Skokie
Phone: 679-9219

Daily, 11:00 A.M.—10:00 P.M.
Closed from Friday at sundown until Saturday at sundown

An Israeli answer to Burger King. Crisp falafel balls (deep-fried, mashed chick peas and spices) are stuffed into hollowed out pita bread along with lettuce, tomato, and tahini (sesame) sauce. It tastes great and is nutritious besides. Cost is 95¢ for a regular falafel and 55¢ for a mini-version. Also shish kabob ($1.50), shawirma (similar to gyros, $1.50), and kifti kabob (ground spiced meat, $1.15). The owner grinds his own meat and everything tastes fresh.

# Garden Gyros

2621 N. Clark
Phone: 935-3100

Daily, 11:00 A.M.—Midnight
Fri.-Sat., 11:00 A.M.—2:00 A.M.

Although everybody's making gyros, Garden Gyros does that and more. Their menu includes a variety of mediterranean sandwiches, all served in pocketed pita bread. There's falafel ($1.25), oregano-spiced kifta kabob ($1.35), and a good hamburger covered with sauteed onions, mushrooms, and green peppers ($1.65).

The owner is Turkish and his repertoire also includes homemade yogurt and the best, creamiest rice pudding (50¢) we've ever tasted. The pudding comes in two flavors—orange (containing slivered orange peel) and chocolate—and the portion is very generous.

## Moveable Feast

1825 N. Lincoln
Phone: 943-6225

Winter:
Mon.-Thur., 10:00 A.M.—10:00 P.M.
Fri., 10:00 A.M.—11:00 P.M.
Sat., 8:30 A.M.—11:00 P.M.;
Sun., 8:30 A.M.—9:00 P.M.
Summer:
Mon.-Thur., 10:00 A.M.—11:00 P.M.
Other days—same as winter

Chicago's longest list of carry-out sandwiches—127 different kinds. Quality varies, and the place could be cleaner. Try good, hefty #66—lox, chive cream cheese, onion, and tomato on a bagel ($1.75) and #67, gefilte fish, horseradish (watch out), tomato, and onion on an onion roll ($1.50). And if you'd like smoked shark meat and cream cheese on whole wheat ($2.45), they've got it. Rattlesnake, too.

## New York Style Pizza, Inc.

5047 N. Lincoln
Phone: 334-4499
914½ Noyes, Evanston
Phone: 864-9400

Tue.-Thur., 11:30 A.M.—Midnight
Fri.-Sat., 4:00 P.M.—1:00 A.M.
Sun., 4:00 P.M.—Midnight
Closed Monday

New York Style brags about making the world's worst pizza (it doesn't), but it might just make the world's best "wedge." Mainly, because we've never tasted another. A wedge tastes something like grilled pizza on French bread and is in reality a grilled submarine. Try the "vegetarian" (mushrooms, onions, peppers, tomatoes, cheese, and tomato sauce) or the "sundance" (sausage, pepperoni, onions, peppers, and cheese). Good eating for $1.30.

Note: A wedge by any other name (at least in Chicago) is a grinder and delicious versions can be found at Eastern Style Pizza (p. 158) and Chicago Pizza and Oven Grinder (p. 157).

## *Resi's Bierstube

2034 W. Irving Park
Phone: 472-1749

Daily, 10:00 A.M.—10:30 P.M.
Fri.-Sat., Noon—10:30 P.M.

A cozy German bar serving fantastic sandwiches and sausages. Open face ham and Swiss cheese on delicious "Cicero" rye ($1.45) can't be beat. Fattest, juiciest thueringer ever, served with sauerkraut and either German potato salad or German fries ($2.25). Good bratwurst too ($2.25). Dark German mustard and horseradish are the condiments.

On weekends, however, the most popular dish is hackepeter (raw ground sirloin, topped with chopped onions, $1.95). One night the man next to us ate five orders.

Steins of Dortmunder for 55¢, and soft pretzels (25¢). Very friendly. Very German. Outdoor beer garden.

# Snacks

# Fish Houses

Chicago may not have the fresh oyster and clam bars or the outdoor crabmeat cocktail stands of coastal cities (wouldn't it be nice,) but we do have some good little places to get seafood. These fisheries range from riverfront shacks to the big and shiny. Besides selling fish (fresh, frozen, and smoked) for home-eating, many offer short-order carry-out snacks, primarily deep-fried fish chips and shrimp.

## Ben's Shrimp House

(Around) 1035 W.
North Ave.
Phone: 337-0263

Tue.-Thur., 9:00 A.M.—11:00 P.M
Fri., 9:00 A.M.—1:00 A.M.
Sat., 11:00 A.M.—1:00 A.M.
Sun., 11:00 A.M.—11:00 P.M.
Closed Monday

A good little riverfront place serving sizzling hot, nugget-sized fish chips in a brown paper bag. Fresh taste; not too heavy breading.

Fish chips—$1.80 (per lb.)
Shrimp—$3.80 (per lb.)

## The Fish House

530 N. Wells
Phone: 642-4158

Daily, 8:00 A.M.—6:00 P.M.
Fri., 8:00 A.M.—7:00 P.M.
Closed Sunday

You need a number here around lunchtime. The place can be packed. Fish chips are nice and crisp, but the coating is a little heavy. For a bargain lunch, try the perch sandwich on a french roll (50¢). The french fried mushrooms (50¢) are an added treat literally exploding in your mouth. Good shrimp too.

Fish chips—$1.80 (per lb.)
Shrimp—$3.40 (per lb.)

## Joe's Fisheries

1438 W. Cortland
Phone: 278-8990

Mon.-Thur., 7:00 A.M.—Midnight
Fri.-Sun.: Open continuously till midnight Sunday

Another riverfront hideaway serving some of the best, meatiest shrimp around. They're medium-sized, and you get a generous amount. Fairly light breading, not greasy. Good, big fish chips too. A popular late-hours place.

Joe's is kind of hard to find. Cortland runs parallel to Armitage (1900 north.)

Fish chips—$2.00 (per lb.)
Shrimp—$4.00 (per lb.)

## Lawrence Fisheries

2120 S. Canal
Phone: 225-2113

Daily, 24 hrs.
Closed holidays

A big, clean carry-out place picturesquely perched beside factories, railroad tracks, and the river. A versatile menu: fish chips, oysters, shrimp, clams, and froglegs. The oysters are especially delicious and cooked to order. Excellent fish chips too.

Fish chips—$1.90 (per lb.)
Shrimp—$3.60 (per lb.)
Oysters—$3.20 (per lb.)
Froglegs—$3.20 (per lb.)
Clams—(prepackaged—$1.25 for a box dinner with french fries, slaw, and roll)

# Health Food and Juice Bars

Chicago just isn't a health food mecca. Hot dogs, ribs, fried chicken, pizza we've got, but just try to find an avocado and sprout sandwich on whole wheat. Getting juiced is much easier, as the city has some fine fruit juice bars.

## Health House Organic Restaurant

36 Main,
Park Ridge
Phone: 696-2992

Lunch, Tue.-Sat., 11:30 A.M.—2:30 P.M.
Dinner, Tue.-Thur., 5:00 P.M.—8:00 P.M.; Fri.-Sat., 5:00 P.M.—10:00 P.M.
Sun., Noon—4:00 P.M.
Closed Monday

An offshot of a big health food store, the restaurant has a phenomenal and somewhat strange menu. Everything from soyburgers ($1.25) to carob milk (40¢). Good salads, twenty-seven different kinds of tea, and health shakes. There's even a special drink for people who need to gain weight, which is made from ice cream, carob, eggs, banana, honey, and peanut butter ($2.25). Wish we could have tried it.

Directions: Take Kennedy to Cumberland. Cumberland north to Touhy. Then east two blocks to Main St. (across from Northwestern Station).

## Organic Munchroom

57 E. Walton
(entrance on Ernst Court)
Phone: 642-2449

Daily, 11:30 A.M.—2:00 P.M.
(Best to call first.)
Closed Wednesday

Located on the 3rd floor of the Yoga Retreat, this tiny, spotless tearoom and bakery offers cookies, muffins, vegetarian soups, and pies in a serene, relaxed setting. Brew your own tea from exotic varieties like Golden Mint, Red Zinger (cherry bark, rosehip, hibiscus, etc.) and a twenty-four herb blend. Hanging plants, fresh flowers. A sanctuary above Rush Street.

# Juice

## Growth and Life

2937 N. Clark
Phone: 929-4272

Tue. & Fri., Noon—7:30 P.M.
Wed. & Thur., Noon—6:30 P.M.
Sat.-Mon., Noon—5:30 P.M.

A nice selection of juices at the rear of this neat little health food store. Mango (50¢, for 8 oz.), papaya (50¢), carrot (60¢), honeydew (60¢), cantaloupe (60¢), and even watermelon (60¢). Snacks include organic ice cream (25¢ a scoop) and an avocado and sprout sandwich on whole wheat ($1.25).

## *Garden Food Products

Illinois Central Station
(Michigan and Randolph)

Mon.-Sat., 7:30 A.M.—9:15 P.M.
Sun., 10:00 A.M.—7:00 P.M.

A hidden oasis for commuters and shoppers. Nestled inconspicuously in the IC station, Garden Food Products offers a staggering variety of juices. Twenty-one flavors in all: guava, mango, black cherry, coconut, passion fruit, apricot, raspberry, strawberry, and more. Exotic combinations too, like Bango Bongo (coconut, mango, and strawberry) and Ol' Smoothie (banana and red cherry). Prices are also smooth. 30¢ for 5 oz.; 40¢ for 8 oz. and 50¢ for 10 oz.

A great place.

## Punch Bowl

Marshall Field and Co.
Randolph and State

Daily, 11:00 A.M.—5:30 P.M.
Closed Sunday

Downtown Chicago's best rest stop—Marshall Field's third floor waiting room. A fine place for people-watching and juice-sipping. The Punch Bowl offers only six flavors, but the raspberry-coconut milk combination (35¢) can't be beat.

## Treasure Island Food Marts

1639 N. Wells
Phone: 642-1105
3460 N. Broadway
Phone: 327-3880
5221 N. Broadway
Phone: 769-3536
2540 W. Lawrence
Phone: 271-8711

Mon.-Fri., 8:00 A.M.—10:00 P.M.
Sat., 8:00 A.M.—8:00 P.M.
Sun., 9:00 A.M.—5:00 P.M.
(Wells St. and Lawrence stores close about an hour earlier.)

Treasure Island does have everything, including a natural fruit juice bar. A great boost for the harried and relaxed shopper alike. The papaya juice is delicious, and you can concoct your own blend, perhaps strawberry and banana. Cost is 45¢ for a 7 oz. glass and 55¢ for a 9 oz. glass.

# Ice Cream Parlors

Despite the popularity of fast service, multiflavor franchises, Chicago still has a fine sampling of old fashioned ice cream parlors. Filled with nostalgia, some of these places haven't changed much since the days of Dobie Gillis, Oogie Pringle, and Judy. Often run by the same family for generations, everything just seems to taste better and richer in these parlors. Probably because most of them still make their own ice cream, toppings, and, sometimes, even whipped cream.

Hopefully, the "real" ice cream parlor will be around for a long time. Here are some great places to indulge:

## The Buffalo

4000 W. Irving Park — Daily, 10:30 A.M.—Midnight
Phone: 725-9488

Nearly another casualty of the oil crisis, The Buffalo was almost doomed to be replaced by a Shell station. Luckily, good sense and community action prevailed and the Buffalo stands, unmolested. At least for another five years.

It's such a grand looking place: heavy wooden booths, mirrors, stained glass, tile floor, and flowery murals of frolicking cherubs. The homemade ice cream is as rich as the decor. Sundaes come with at least two big scoops, a lavish dollop of hand-beaten whipped cream, and Nabiscos. Some add chopped nuts and bananas.

Try a hot fudge with the works (pecans and bananas, $1.05), a caramel walnut sundae ($1.00), or a hot fudge marshmallow ($1.00). Also good are the fresh (frozen) strawberry or raspberry sundaes (95¢). Very chocolately chocolate sodas (65¢) and thick shakes and malts (65¢).

A great place for ice cream, but expect to wait in line and maybe sit in the modern adjoining room, especially in the summer.

A second Buffalo opened recently at 6000 W. Dempster, Morton Grove (Phone: 966-2426).

## *Dr. Jazz

1607 W. Montrose
Phone: 477-7199

Summer Hours:
(June-Sept.)
Daily, 4:00 P.M.—Midnight
Fri., 4:00 P.M.—1:00 A.M.
Sat., 1:00 P.M.—1:00 A.M.
Sun., 1:00 P.M.—11:00 P.M.
Non-Summer Hours:
Daily, 7:00 P.M.—11:00 P.M.
Fri.-Sat., 7:00 P.M.—1:00 A.M.
Sun., 1:00 A.M.—11:00 P.M.

Dr. Jazz has to be the happiest place in Chicago, sure to cure any form of urban blues. Although a relative newcomer to the ice cream scene, it's so steeped in nostalgia that you'd never know it. It's dazzling—a combination fun house, antique store, and fantasy trip. The booths are candy apple red, hanging ceiling fans whir, antique toys, and amusement park games are everywhere, not to mention two musical marvels—a machine (PianOrchestrion) that plays thirteen instruments at once and another, the violano, that is an amazing marriage of violin and piano. Silent movies too, at 8:00, 9:00 and 10:00 P.M.

With all this, who needs ice cream? But it's here and excellent (not homemade), even though prices are becoming far from old fashioned. Terrific sodas (75¢), big sundaes ($1.19), and the best peanut butter milk shake (99¢) in town. Green River Floats (85¢) and a fresh orange cream (fresh orange juice blended with ice cream, 85¢) too.

Really packed on weekends. And there's now a second Dr. Jazz at 4059 W. North. (Phone: 276-4000).

## Gayety Ice Cream Parlor

9207 S. Commercial
Phone: 734-8867

Daily, 9:00 A.M.—10:00 P.M.

The days of hanging out at the soda shop after school are long gone, but the Gayety still looks like the place where it happened. Even though most of their business is now carry-out, the flavor isn't gone—especially of the ice cream. It's homemade, so are the toppings and even the whipped cream.

Sundaes, among them a fresh-tasting raspberry, maplenut, and caramel nut are 60¢. Sodas and shakes (try a banana shake) are 55¢ and a hot fudge split is 80¢. Ice cream cones are only 15¢.

The owner barks orders at his young workers, who should be applauded for dishing out fantastic concoctions in the smallest work space imaginable. Take out orders are huge and slightly higher priced.

## Ideal Candy Shop

3311 N. Clark
Phone: 327-2880

Mon.-Sat., 11:00 A.M.—9:30 P.M.
Sun., 11:00 A.M.—5:00 P.M.
Closed Tuesday

Located at the same Clark Street address for thirty-eight years, Ideal still retains the appearance and personal feeling of the past. Elaborately wrapped, rainbow-colored boxes of candy, all-day suckers, neat rows of rich chocolates, and stuffed toys hold reign. But you can still dig into ice cream at the tiny counter in the back. Good homemade hot fudge and hot butterscotch splits (85¢). Although Ideal doesn't make its own ice cream, cubes of good, creamy Highlanders are used. Regular sundaes are 60¢ and sodas are 55¢. Malts and milk shakes come in three sizes—heavy, extra heavy, and super heavy (60¢–70¢–80¢). They also make the best caramel apples (30¢) around, sticky with thick homemade caramel.

It's a neat little place, with memories enough to carry you right back to the summer of '36.

## *Gertie's Ice Cream Parlor

5858 S. Kedzie
Phone: 737-9634

Daily, 10:30 A.M.—11:00 P.M.
Fri.-Sat., 10:30 A.M.—11:30 P.M.

The oldest of our ice cream parlors (1901) and a great one. Quality is superlative. In season, they make a fresh strawberry soda that is the real thing—lots of big, fresh strawberry halves (80¢). A great strawberry sundae (80¢) too.

Regular sundaes and sodas are 70¢, but we like to splurge a little with a caramel or banana milkshake (80¢), hot fudge sundae with pecans (90¢), or tin roof sundae (Dutch chocolate sauce and peanuts, 90¢). Also, there are fancier sundaes with valentine names like Lover's Delight ($1.00) and Sweet Sixteen ($1.00).

An old time, comfortable place with plush purple-cushioned booths and some of the biggest, gaudiest stuffed animals this side of Riverview. The owner can be a little gruff, but his homemade ice cream is wonderful. It's available for carryout at 90¢ a quart, and flavors include fresh banana, peppermint, and maple-walnut.

## *Margie's Candies

Corner of Armitage & Western Daily, 7:00 A.M.—1:30 A.M.
Phone: 384-1035

Run by a pleasantly eccentric woman, Margie's makes what have to be the most generous hot fudge and hot caramel sundaes around. The superb homemade sauces are served separately in silver containers, and there's not only enough topping to thoroughly cover your ice cream, but some left over to eat by itself. A luxury for 90¢.

Fruit sundaes, peach, raspberry, and banana, cost 85¢, and so do Boston sodas. Margie also claims the world's largest sundae ($5.00). Ice cream's from Highlander, but the whipped cream is homemade.

Margie's is filled with a profusion of stuffed animals, plastic flowers, and plants, and has stood on the same corner since 1925. It's not a beauty, but what fantastic sundaes!

## Peacock's Dairy Bar

626 Davis, Evanston
Phone: 864-4904
100 Skokie Boulevard, Wilmette
Phone: 251-4141

Daily: 11:00 A.M.—Midnight

Peakcock's makes eighteen flavors (including green mint, cinnamon, chocolate almond, coconut, and, in summer, a fabulous fresh peach) of incredibly rich ice cream. Any flavor may be used in their sodas (99¢) and sundaes (99¢). A good place for a coffee soda with coffee ice cream. There are creme de menthe, black raspberry, and burgundy cherry sundaes, as well as a very generous hot fudge. Cooling raspberry or pineapple fruit freezes for 79¢.

Peacock's is big, bright, and airy, and serves sandwiches too.

# Italian Lemonade

When the discomfort index starts moving above 80°, there's not much to do besides moan, sit in a bathtub, air-conditioned closet, or have an Italian lemonade. If you opt for the latter, it's a slushy mixture of fresh chopped lemon (peels and all), smoothly crushed ice, and sugar. Good lemonade is made on the spot in a special Italian lemonade machine (although as the old machines break down, places are switching to soft ice cream machines, with good results).

Lemonade stands open and close with the robins and the Cubs. You can generally count on finding at least one in business from early April til early October. Prices of lemonade go up according to size, and can range from 5¢ to $2.75 for a gallon (to keep in the freezer for emergencies.)

Lemonade stands generally open at around ten in the morning and stay open til at least ten at night (later, if weather's hot.) Although there aren't many real lemonade stands left, here are a few good ones:

## Carm's

1057 W. Polk

Good, very smooth lemonade at this little Taylor Street-area stand. They also dish out beef sandwiches and subs. They'll stay open at least til midnight if it's good and hot out. Usually crowded on a summer evening.

## *Mario and Donna's

1068 W. Taylor

Not far from Carm's, this tiny stand is a classic. They only serve lemonade and sno-cones. Very icy-textured lemonade made in an old machine. They add flavors here and the lemonade with fresh watermelon chunks is indescribably good. Interesting street scene and tortilla factory next door.

## *Romano's

1136 W. Armitage

Great lemonade—smooth, usually lots of lemon chunks, good flavor. Romano's is probably our favorite. Recently switched to the new machine, but the product is just as good. They also sell Italian beef sandwiches, etc.

## Tito's

1901 S. California

In a hidden corner of Chicago (underneath some railroad tracks)—a family-run trio of businesses: lemonade stand, beef and sausage stand, and open-air fresh fruit set-up. Picnic tables too. If the lemonade were bad (and it isn't,) this place would be worth coming to for atmosphere alone. It's neighborhood Chicago at its best.

# Pastry and Coffee

Where better to relax than at a cafe serving good coffee, tea, and pastries. We've included five particularly nice ones: two German, one Greek, one a continental combination, and one that could best be categorized as early-sixties coffee house.

## Cafe Pergolisi

3404 N. Halsted
Phone: 472-8602

Daily, 8:00 P.M.—1:00 A.M.
Fri.-Sat., 8:00 P.M.—2:00 A.M.
Sunday brunch: 10:00 A.M.—3:00 P.M.

Among the last of a vanishing breed. A subdued coffee house in the classic tradition—espresso machines, chess sets, lots of conversation, and classical music. A place to relax and enjoy.

Coffee (espresso, cappuccino, mocha, anise, etc.), tea (fourteen different kinds, including gunpowder and sassafras), and delicious hot chocolate (try the mint chocolate for a real treat). Also, cinnamon cider, lemonade, tamarindo with lemon, and more. Prices range from 40¢ to a $1.00.

The primary pastry is a good, sticky cheesecake (70¢). Interesting, but doll-sized sundaes ($1.00). But where else could you find kumquat sauce?

## Kenessey Gourmet Internationale

403 W. Belmont
Phone: 929-7500
1100 S. Elmhurst Road, Mt. Prospect
Phone: 437-8500
Parking: In Chicago, free parking with doorman at Belmont Hotel

Daily, 11:00 A.M.—11:00 P.M.
Sat., 11:00 A.M.—Midnight
Sun., Noon—9:00 P.M.

Display case stocked with dark chocolate tortes (55¢), eclairs filled with either custard or whipped cream (60¢), cherry, cheese, poppyseed, and apple strudels (70¢), lemon cream rolls (60¢), apricot turnovers (40¢), almond crescents (60¢), and much more. A beautiful sight. Delicious eating. Excellent coffee (35¢), espresso (60¢), cappuccino (75¢), hot chocolate with whipped cream (50¢), and Kenessey's special (coffee with brandy or rum, $2.00).

Small tables set up so you can leisurely savor it all. No place for a diet, but a great spot to break one. Carry-outs, also.

Downstairs is a gourmet grocery, cheese, and wine cellar. Good, but slightly expensive, open-face sandwiches. Taste their special whipped Hungarian cream cheese.

## Konditorei Kleinert

4701 N. Lincoln
Phone: 728-5917

Daily, 9:00 A.M.—10:00 P.M.
Closed Monday

A less stuffy Lutz's. Caters primarily to neighborhood Germans. Immaculate, pleasant, not as uptight. Rather gaudy, Hollywood-style decor.

Good mixed fruit (mandarin orange, pineapple, and strawberry) and fresh strawberry tortes (50¢), poppyseed or cherry slices with struesel topping (50¢), almond butterhorns (45¢), etc. Fine coffee. Tea served in little pots. Dainty open-face sandwiches (Wesphalian ham, liver sausage, salami, 95¢) too.

If you choose not to sit, any of the pastries are available for carry-out at slightly less expensive prices.

## Lutz's

2454 W. Montrose
Phone: 478-7785

Tues.-Sun., 11:00 A.M.—10:00 P.M.
Closed Monday

A most proper German cafe, serving very exuberant pastries. 75¢ will buy a lovely light whipped cream torte: rich chocolate dobosh, sacher, schwarzwalder cherry, brandy trifle, etc. Our favorites, however, are the fruit kuchens, especially the fresh plum (available in fall only). The rich dough is loaded with fruit, and tastes unbelievably good.

Expensive sandwiches and fancy sundaes also available. In summer, dine outdoors in a beautiful flowered patio.

Don't plan on Lutz's unless you have nothing to lose, because even the coffee's served with whipped cream.

Carry-outs available, in bustling front room.

## Melissa

2609 W. Lawrence
Phone: 271-0292

Daily, 8:00 A.M.—1:00 A.M.

A lively, glossy-looking coffee house that literally buzzes with sound. Filled primarily with young Greek men, with at least a dozen animated conversations going on at once.

Good Greek pastries too, from a syrupy baclava (50¢) to rolled, deep-fried diples (50¢) to almond pyramids (65¢). The galactoboureco (farina-based pudding covered with thin filo dough and sugar syrup) is excellent and served warm (50¢). But the real star is rizogalo, or Greek rice pudding (65¢). It's rich and creamy, beautifully-flavored with orange peel and whole cinnamon sticks.

American coffee (35¢), thick Greek coffee (45¢), and lemonade (50¢) for drinking. You're welcome to sit for hours —everybody does.

# Pizza

We think Chicago has the best pizza in the United States. In fact we've never had a pizza outside these environs that could even compare with Chicago's second rate places. And being pizza freaks, don't think we haven't tried. In recent years, thick crust pizza in the pan has more or less taken over thin crust turf. The following list, though far from exclusive, includes the best of both. Because of a variety of sizes and ingredients, prices given, where applicable, are for large cheese and sausage pizza.

## Chicago Pizza and Oven Grinder Co.

2121 N. Clark
Phone: 248-2570

Daily, 5:00 P.M.—11:00 P.M.
Fri.-Sat., 5:00 P.M.—2:00 A.M.
Sun., 4:00 P.M.—11:00 P.M.

Not a pizza for purists—more like a casserole. Pizza sold by the pound, at $3.25 per pound (a one-pounder feeds one person but a two-pounder feeds 2 to 3). Excellent sauce made with plum tomatoes, lots of mild cheese, sausage, peppers, onions, and whole fresh mushrooms. Good crust, good quality, but keeps getting higher-priced. Fantastic grinders ($3.00)—glorified baked submarine sandwiches featuring meatballs, sausage, ham, or salami with tomato sauce, melted cheese, and trimmings. Also great mountainous salads. Several Italian wines available and full bar. Somewhat pretentious but attractive place, catering to a young crowd. Often a wait. No carry-outs.

## Eastern Style Pizza

2911 W. Touhy
Phone: 761-4070
465-9659

Daily, 11:30 A.M.—Midnight
Fri.-Sat., 11:30 A.M.—1:00 A.M.
Sunday, 4:00 P.M.—Midnight

This is the home of the pizza with everything. Your $2.70 will buy a super pizza (serves 2) that has to be eaten to be understood. A medium thick, crisp crust is showered with pepperoni, sausage, salami, bacon, meatballs, shrimp, mushrooms, peppers, onions, anchovies (optional), and, of course, cheese. If this doesn't sound intriguing you can always opt for a plain mushroom, sausage, or any of the above ($1.90). Also home of the original grinders. Carry-outs only.

There's also an Eastern Style in Niles at the Golf Mill Shopping Center (827-0193).

## Gino's East

160 E. Superior
Phone: 943-1168 (upstairs)
943-1124 (downstairs)

Daily, 11:00 A.M.—2:00 A.M.
Sat., 11:00 A.M.—3:00 A.M.
Sun.. 4:00 P.M.—1:30 A.M.

There's good pizza in the pan right off Michigan Ave. Best thing about Gino's offering is the outstanding crust—flaky, crisp, never doughy, delicious. The extra ingredients (like the sausage) are chopped fine, so that the whole topping kind of melts in together. $4.95 for a large cheese and sausage. Carry-outs available. Tasty.

Two places to indulge: upstairs—plush, chandliered, and filled with businessmen; downstairs—dark and collegiate, lots of young medical students. Apt to be crowded, even during the day.

## *Home Run Inn

4251 W. 31st
Phone: 247-9696
247-9475

Daily, 11:00 A.M.—1:30 A.M.
Sat., 11:00 A.M.—2:30 A.M.
Sun., Noon—1:00 A.M.

South Side's most popular pizza place and best thin crust pizza in the city. Busy, bustling, down-home kind of place. Thin, rich-crusted pizza that's piled with mushrooms, peppers, onions, or whatever extras you fancy. Cheesy, gooey, slightly oily—it's good old fifties pizza parlor style. Two rooms—one slick and modern; the other older and funkier with long bar and great "dogs at a dance" wallpaper. Large cheese and sausage is $4.60. Carry-outs available.

## Lou Malnati's

6649 N. Lincoln,
Lincolnwood
Phone: 673-0800

Daily, 11:00 A.M.—1:00 A.M.
Sat., Noon—2:00 A.M.
Sun., 3:00 P.M.—Midnight

A sprawling pizza parlor with an avid following. The multi-roomed restaurant is usually packed with north side families because they make a pizza with pizzazz. Biggest pluses—crunchy, moderately-thick crust and a bountiful showering of ingredients. Exceptionally generous with their mild-flavored sausage. Not super cheesy. Large cheese and sausage at $5.50. Carry-outs available.

Also a second Lou Malnati's at 1050 East Higgins in Elk Grove Village (phone: 439-2000).

## Nite n' Gale

346 Waukegan, Highwood
Phone: 432-9744

Daily, 11:00 A.M.—3:00 P.M.; 4:00 P.M.—Midnight
Sun., 4:00 P.M.—Midnight

For years had a well-deserved reputation for its excellent thin crust pizza. Recently made the switch to fat crust with equally successful results. Fresh-tasting crisp crust (occasionally it can be *too* thick), subtle tomato sauce with tomato bits, and a magnificent mass of melted cheese. When it's good, it's really good. Large cheese and sausage, $5.25. Carry-outs available.

Nite n' Gale is housed in large pseudo-medieval English dining rooms. Also serves tasty ribs and a good ½ lb. hamburger on rye ($1.95).

Directions: Take Edens Expressway to Route 22 (Half Day Rd.). Go east to dead end. Turn left. Go one block and turn right, cross train tracks and then turn left ½ block to Nite n' Gale. Good luck.

## Pequod's

8520 Fernald,
Morton Grove
Phone: 967-9161

Mon.-Fri., 11:00 A.M.—2:00 P.M.
Tue.-Thur., and Sun.: 4:00 P.M.—Midnight
Fri.-Sat., 4:00 P.M.—1:00 A.M.

Named for a ship, located in a house, and filled with a fantastic collection of antique radios, Pequod's is not your average pizza place. They do make a mighty fine pan pizza. Fresh tasting, cheesy, on the mild side, and served sizzling hot. One slight fault—the crust is sometimes too bread-like. A large cheese and sausage is $5.00.

An amiable young couple run it and go all out to make you enjoy yourself (even serving after-dinner mints.) Very casual. Very nice.

Directions: Take Edens to Dempster West Exit. Follow Dempster to Fernald (about 6200 west). Turn right at Fernald, about 3 blocks to Pequod's.

## Pizzaria Due

619 N. Wabash
Phone: 943-2400

Daily, 11:30 A.M.—3:00 A.M.
Sat., 5:00 P.M.—4:00 A.M.
Closed Sunday

One of Chicago's two sister pizza emporiums, and in our opinion, much the better of the two (though Uno's has a homier atmosphere.) Always crowded, but you can call in and order your pizza in advance. One of the original proponents of pizza in the pan. Crisp, thick crust topped with spicy blend of cheese, tomatoes, and sausage. Not super rich or greasy. Large cheese and sausage is $5.00. Carry-outs available.

## *Ria's

3943 N. Lincoln
Phone: 281-8812

Daily: 4:00 P.M.—Midnight
Fri.-Sat., 4:00 P.M.—1:00 A.M.

Ria's makes a fabulous pizza, which we generally concede to be our favorite. It's mainly the sausage. They lay it on thick, it's homemade and pleasantly spicy with just a hint of orange peel. The crust is medium thick, rich, and flaky. Sauce contains pieces of tomato, a healthy helping of oregano and a fine amount of melted cheese. All works together in producing a pizza that one inevitably dreams about at one in the morning on the road in the middle of Wyoming.

Ria's has full bar service and looks unmistakably like countless other restaurant-lounges throughout America. Large cheese and sausage, $4.95. Carry-outs and delivery available, within a reasonable distance.

## Ricobene's

250 W. 26th
Phone: 225-9811

Daily, 11:00 A.M.—12:30 P.M.
Fri.-Sat., 11:00 A.M.—2:00 P.M.
Sun., 5:00 P.M.—Midnight

Located in the shadow of a hulking expressway, Ricobene's must be Chicago's noisiest pizza place. It also does a nonstop business because the pizza's terrific. It's thin-crusted, has cheese that won't quit and fat chunks of mild, good quality sausage. This is strictly an open air carry-out operation, so you might want to call in your order ahead of time. Interesting neighborhood scene. For a surreal experience, try eating in the playground across the street, directly under the freeway. Large cheese and sausage, $4.30.

Directions: Located a half block west of Wentworth, just south of Chinatown.

## Salerno's

6633 W. 16th, Berwyn
Phone: 484-3400

Daily, 10:00 A.M.—1:00 A.M.
Sat., 10:00 A.M.—2:00 A.M.
Sun., Noon—Midnight

Big, popular, multi-roomed Berwyn pizza parlor (and restaurant.) They serve a medium thick-crusted pizza. One of the cheesiest we've come across—enough cheese to strangle you. Mildly spicy. Pizzas range in size from a baby to an extra-large, and they're not kidding. Large cheese and sausage, $4.85. Carry-outs available.

# Pizza by the Slice

Chicago has several places where you can snack on a slice (or two or three) of pizza. Pizza slices can be bought primarily in bakeries, though some restaurants and sandwich shops also sell it. Here are a few:

## The Bread Shop

3400 N. Halsted
Phone: 528-8108

Daily, 5:30 A.M.—6:30 P.M.
Sun., 11:00 A.M.—5:00 P.M.
Closed Monday

The healthiest pizza in town. All natural ingredients from bottom to top. Whole wheat crust and topping of tomato sauce, carrots, zucchini, mushrooms, onions, green pepper, celery, and raw milk cheese. Not only good for you, but good-tasting. Sometimes they even make a pizza with a brown rice topping. 50¢ a slice.

## De Leo's Bakery

1119 W. Taylor St.
Phone: 421-9352

Go in the morning
Closed Sunday

Much like a pizzabread—rich and tomato sauced. Not for cheese freaks. They cut each slice with a scissors. 30¢ a slice.

## John's Jumbo Sandwich Shop

1955 W. Grand
Phone: 421-9814

Daily, 10:00 A.M.—11:30 P.M.
Closed Sunday

A workingman's sandwich shop. Crowded at lunch when everyone feasts on beef, sausage, meatball sandwiches, spaghetti, etc. But you can also get a warm slice of pizza to snack on. 35¢ a slice.

## The Original Sicilian Bakery

3962 W. Grand
Phone: 252-9186

Daily, 9:00 A.M.—7:00 P.M.
Sundays, 9:00 A.M.—2:00 P.M.

Authentic little bakery, selling a moderately spicy, fine slice of pizza (20¢ apiece.) Also delicious cannoli with candied fruit and chocolate chips hidden in the filling (30¢).

## Scafuri Bakery

1337 W. Taylor
Phone: 733-8881

Go in the morning
Closed Sunday

Very similar to De Leo's. Tomato predominates in this breadlike pizza. Best to get here early when pizza's warm, and they're sure to have some. 25¢ a slice.

# Miscellaneous Snacks

If you're looking for something different, perhaps exotica like Chinese dim sum or merely a good bowl of chili, Chicago's got it. Scan this list, and maybe you'll hit upon something you've had a craving for.

## Bishop's Chili Hut

1958 W. 18th — Mon.-Sat., 9:00 A.M.—7:30 P.M.
Phone: 829-6345 — Closed Sunday
7220 W. Roosevelt — Mon.-Sat., 9:00 A.M.—1:00 A.M.
Phone: 366-4421 — Sun., Noon—Midnight
250 W. Cass, Westmont — Mon.-Sat., 9:00 A.M.—1:00 A.M.
Phone: 852-5974 — Sun., Noon—9:00 P.M.

The place to go for chili and chili mac. 80¢ a bowl, and lots of oyster crackers and hot pepper sauce on the side, though the chili's pretty peppy on its own. Wash it down with a stein of beer. Casual, friendly places. Also, chili to go (fresh or frozen).

## Le Cordon Bleu, Inc.

3243 N. Broadway — Tue.-Sat., 10:00 A.M.—7:30 P.M.
Phone: 248-2738 — Sun., 10:00 A.M.—6:00 P.M.
Closed Monday

If you'd like an apricot tart (50¢) or a ham, bacon, and cheese quiche (60¢) to munch while you walk, stop in at Le Cordon Bleu. Primarily a gourmet French catering and carry-out-dinner service, they also offer several snacks to eat on the run. Among them, napoleons, fruit tarts, several kinds of quiches, and salmon en croute. Look in their red display cases and pick out whatever pleases.

## *Garrett Popcorn Shop

10 W. Madison
Phone: 263-8466

Daily, 9:30 A.M.—Midnight
Sun., Noon—10:00 P.M.

Garrett's starts your mouth watering as soon as you enter the door. Could a rose smell as sweet as freshly popped caramel corn? Prices range from 15¢ for a small bag up to $1.90 for a twenty-ounce sack. Also fresh popcorn, cheese popcorn, popcorn balls, and fudge.

## Happy Garden Bakery

2358 S. Wentworth
Phone: 225-2730

Daily, 9:00 A.M.—7:00 P.M.
Closed Tuesday

Located at the far south end of Chinatown, this little bakery specializes in fresh baked dim sum (Chinese tea pastries). Good smells. Some unusual tastes. Especially nice are the soft buns filled with coconut and peanut butter. Also cha shu bow (buns filled with barbequed pork), ham and egg filled buns, a flaky pastry containing curried chicken, and almond cookies.

## House of Eggroll

3303 N. Marshfield
Phone: 281-7888

Daily, 11:00 A.M.—10:00 P.M.

It's hard to pass up a place called House of Eggroll. Six different varieties are offered, including chicken, ham, beef, barbequed pork, shrimp and pork, and vegetable, priced from 60¢ to 75¢. They're good sized, crisp-skinned, and make a great snack. Also on the menu, bite-sized, steamed, open-topped won ton (three pieces for 65¢) and fried chicken (!).

## Matina's

4020½ S. California
Phone: 254-2849

Daily, 10:00 A.M.—7:00 P.M.
Sunday, 10:00 A.M.—5:00 P.M.

Would you believe chocolate covered watermelon? Matina's makes up a batch each summer, if the price of watermelon isn't up too high. If it is, they also sell good chocolate-dipped bananas, homemade caramel apples, candied orange slices, spearmint leaves, big gumdrops, and red juju coins in this tiny, charming little candy shop.

## RR Western Restaurant and Lounge

56 W. Madison
Phone: 263-8207

Daily, 11:00 A.M.—3:00 A.M.

Something different. A cowboy bar in downtown Chicago featuring country music (after 8:00 P.M.) and thirty variations of chili and chili-based sandwiches. It's darker than a side street inside, but once you adjust there's much to see—a vast gun display, bleached steerskulls, ten gallon hats, etc.

The basic chili (84¢) and chili mac ($1.19) are thick and spicy, and there are also more far-flung variations like chili mac cheese tamale ($1.52) and chili perch (ugh!)

# In a Class of Their Own

## *Maxwell Street

1300 south, at Halsted    Sundays only: Anywhere from 5:00 A.M.—Noon

The best place for all-out, anything-goes, street snacking. Chicago's oldest and funkiest open air market. Walk around Maxwell Street on a Sunday morning, and the aromas will knock you out. Sizzling ribs and pork chops, Polish sausages smothered with onions, shredded beef tacos prepared while you wait, and maybe even a group of Hungarians frying pancake-sized doughnuts. There's a guy selling home canned fruit that looks like it was left over from the Civil War. The fruit we wouldn't recommend, but everything else is fine.

Colorful characters. Great music. And if you need some used nuts and bolts, shoelaces, snake oil . . .

## *Chicago Folk Fair

Held at Navy Pier, usually the first weekend in November.

The ethnic eating extravaganza of the year. A tribute to Chicago's melting pot diversity. Food, crafts, and folk dancing are on display. The food section alone stretches for a good half-mile. Edibles from dozens of nationalities are represented, much of it prepared while you watch. What a feast! There's Ghanian peanut stew, Pakistani roast lamb with rice pilaf, Native American fried bread and pumpkin pudding, Norwegian open face sandwiches, Latvian apple fritters, and a mind-boggling amount of strudels, breads, and assorted pastry. Last year Chef Louis of The Bakery was even preparing Hungarian palascinta (crêpes) for 20¢ each! Prices for everything are minimal and furthermore, admission is free. A must!

# A Few Bites More

ALICIA #2, 852 N. Ashland (421-9798)
Tiny place with elaborate decor and authentic Mexican food. Delicious, messy tostadas de carnitas (thin sliced pork). Good pork stew with salsa verde (green sauce).

LAS AMERICAS, 3723 N. Southport (477-2990)
Neighborhood Mexican restaurant serving delicious juicy tacos and really hot guacamole. Clean and nice.

ARVEY'S, 7041 W. Oakton, Niles (967-9790)
Great place for a Wednesday night bash. Dinners include saganaki (flaming cheese pie), egg-lemon soup, and a big helping of Caesar salad. Mostly Greek entrees, but there's also an inexpensive steak Diane ($3.95) and a broiled skirt steak (3.95).

BLUE PEACOCK, 2340 W. Devon (761-5050)
Large, interesting Chinese menu. Try delicate crab rangoon appetizer. Excellent sweet and sour won ton, hong sue chicken and pepper beef.

BOHEMIA, 6026 W. Cermak, Cicero (863-9297)
Yet another low-priced neighborhood Bohemian restaurant. Old-fashioned ambience. Most dinners under $3.00, including incredibly juicy, crisp roast duck.

BUCKET OF SUDS, 3123 N. Cicero (283-9485)
A unique local bar that has the biggest liquor collection we've ever seen and features Italian homecooking by the owner's sister.

BUSY BEE, 1546 N. Damen (384-8775)
Lives up to its name, especially at lunch. Good Polish food in an old fashioned setting. Delicious thueringer and knackwurst with kraut ($1.80).

CAFE RAUL, 939 W. Webster
Mexican restaurant/bar that serves a generous portion of really good flautas.

CHARLIE'S, 2201 W. Montrose (588-9470)
A typical corner coffee shop that you'd never guess served Middle Eastern food. But they do, and it's good, especially the homemade yogurt. Falafel, kibbi, too. Ask for the special menu.

THE DUMPLING HOUSE, 4109 S. Harlem, Stickney (484-9633)
Bohemian families on a night out. Big meals under $3.00. Crisp pork tenderloin and smoky-flavored sauerkraut.

EDITH'S BAR-B-QUE, 1863 N. Clybourn (327-5160)
Friendly, neat little barbeque spot where slabs of ribs are leisurely smoked over hickory logs. The ribs are meaty, juicy, messy, and a definite treat for $3.95 (half-slabs, $2.50). Crisp fried chicken and fish too.

FAR EAST RESTAURANT, 510 W. Diversey (935-6550)
Reliable Chinese food. Above average won ton soup, gai chow won ton, and chicken pineapple. Huge portions.

GIOVANNETTI'S, 216 N. Wabash, (322-9503)
Convenient downtown restaurant/bar with varied Italian menu. Tasty lasagna. Experienced, "old school" waiters. Jammed at lunch, nice for dinner.

GLASS DOME HICKORY PIT, 2724 S. Union (842-7600)
In the Mayor's neighborhood. They're known for their ribs, but the fried chicken's even better. Definitely finger-licking good.

EL GRAN COLOMBIA, 3908 N. Lincoln (281-4460)
Specialties from Colombia. The paella ($11 for two) is terrific. Other food varies. A promising, but not always reliable place. Good music on weekends.

HARRIS RESTAURANT, 3148 W. Irving Park (539-2357)
A sterile coffee shop complete with muzak where the food is actually good. Homey-tasting roast chicken. And they bake their own hot apple pie, strawberry cheesecake, strawberry tart, etc. Open twenty-four hours.

HOLIDAY GRILL, 1402 W. Belmont
Mainly for breakfast. Down home southern cooking: grits, cornbread, biscuits, and gravy.

HOUSE OF YAKITORI, 3023 N. Broadway (929-9050)
Home of Japanese-style shish kabobs—small skewers of grilled chicken, beef, shrimp, or vegetables. Cost is 33¢ to 53¢ a skewer. Teriyaki-like flavor. Nice for snacking in New Town.

KAI KAI, 2218 S. Wentworth (225-1952)
Chinatown restaurant popular with local Chinese residents. Very cheap. Delicious fried rice.

LA LINTERNA VERDE, 4205 N. Broadway (281-9705)
Chicago's only Argentine restaurant. Food preparation uneven, but there's an interesting broiled steak, Argentine-style.

THE MAGGIE, 1447 W. Devon (743-9251)
A charming little restaurant with a broad range of specialties from the British Isles. Everything from kippers and eggs to stewed rhubarb and cream. Good fish n' chips, fried tomatoes, apple fritters. Brewed tea. Clancy Brothers and Mattie Toohy on the jukebox.

EL MEXICANO, 2627 N. Clark (528-2131)
An offshoot of a bowling alley. Potent chile rellenos and good enchiladas, especially the cheesy enchiladas suiza. Dependable, unpretentious.

MEXICO TAQUERIA, 1350 S. Halsted (733-9295) or 7604 N. Ashland (338-1473)

Some of the cheapest Mexican food in town. Especially tasty tostadas suiza, garnachas (tortilla chips covered with beans and melted cheese), and combination plates. Open twenty-four hours.

MUSHROOM & SONS, LTD., 1825 Second St., Highland Park (432-0824)

Greenery galore. Twenty different salad combinations with a choice of homemade dressings. Try the fresh mushroom, raw cauliflower, or fruit. Some fine hot dishes too, particularly brown rice and vegetables. Also "health" sandwiches and deli-type selections.

PALANGA, 6918 S. Western (476-9758)

Friendly neighborhood Lithuanian restaurant. Robust soups, superb bread, and crisp duck ($3.00).

PANCAKE FRANCAIS, 506 Davis St., Evanston (475-8810)

A fresh, cheerful crêperie. Good, delicate dessert crêpes, including an unusual grapefruit version. Accompany with strong chicory coffee.

PATRIA, 2011 W. North (686-6565)

Quiet Polish restaurant. Big menu, daily specials, even a salad bar. Fat, chewy pierogi.

LA POSADA, 2601 S. Ridgeway (762-9818)

Popular with Mexican families. Homemade flour tortillas kept in a warmer at your table. Spicy mole sauce, juicy tacos. Big portions, low prices.

PEACOCK'S HILLTOP RESTAURANT, 79 E 103rd (821-6315)

Lively soul food restaurant. Super cheap. Three side dishes with entree. Sweet peach cobbler for dessert.

SHALIMAR, 2650 N. Clark (750-2322)

Self-service style Indian restaurant. Varied menu. Tandoori specialties and good vegetable dishes. Carry-outs available.

TREFFPUNKT, 4743 N. Lincoln (784-9296)

A spirited German restaurant/bar. Generous servings. Excellent sauerbraten, liver dumpling soup, and farmer's breakfast (a puffy omelette filled with potatoes and ham). Accordian music from Wednesday to Sunday.

TWIN ANCHORS, 1655 N. Sedgwick (944-9714)

A local bar in the Old Town area with a mighty reputation for its barbecued ribs. At $3.75, an excellent buy. Good hamburger too.

TWO GUYS FROM ITALY, 50 Highwood Avenue, Highwood (432-2889)

Dishes vary, but linguine with clam sauce is a standout.

VILLA GIRGENTI, 7625 N. Paulina (743-9872)

The place for a meatball sandwich. Big, sloppy, delicious. The eggplant parmigiana's not bad either.

WELTY'S, 130 S. Clark (332-0477)

If you're downtown on a Friday, stop in for their superb red snapper soup.

YERUSHALAIM, 2901 W. Devon (262-2854)

Israeli-kosher restaurant. Coffee shop atmosphere. Folksy food. Entrees range from boiled chicken to shish kabob. Good stuffed cabbage.

ZUM DEUTSCHEN ECK, 2924 N. Southport (525-8121)

Consistent food. Comfortable setting. Healthy portions of German favorites—sauerbraten, wiener schnitzel, beef rouladan, schweinshaxen (pork shank), etc. Most dinners range from $3.50 to $4.50. Costumed waitresses and sing-a-longs on weekends.

# Location Index

## Loop and Near North



## Mid North

## Far North



## Northwest

## Near West



## West



## South



## Southwest

## Suburbs

# Alphabetical Index

# The Good But Cheap

# Chicago Restaurant Newsletter

We're starting a monthly newsletter. It will focus on new "finds", detailed restaurant reviews, and any significant changes in previously included restaurants.

We'll cover specific nationalities (Serbian, Thai, Mexican, Italian, etc.), special categories of food (best ribs in town, where to find a decent salad, richest cheesecake, etc.), and specialty shops (butchers, bakers and candy makers). We'll report on everything from early breakfasts to late night snacks. In addition we'll keep you up to date on important ethnic food festivals. Sometimes we'll venture out of the city and suburbs altogether and find out what's cooking in the country.

If you'd like to take part in this eating adventure, we offer 10 food-filled issues for $4 a year.

We invite you to mail your address and a check to:
The Good But Cheap Chicago Restaurant Newsletter
P.O. Box A3963
Chicago, Illinois 60690

Dear Reader

If you think that we've left any good restaurants out, or included some that you feel should be omitted in the future, let us know. We'd really appreciate it. Just fill in the postcard and drop it in the mail.

Please include:

Name of restaurant ______________________
Address ______________________
Type of food served ______________________
Favorite dish ______________________
Price range ______________________
Other comments ______________________
______________________
______________________
______________________

Next time Forget About:

Name of restaurant ______________________
Comments ______________________
______________________
______________________
______________________

Mail to: The Good But Cheap Chicago Restaurant Book
P.O. Box A3963
Chicago, Illinois 60690

Gejalt's —
on arrivage
out of doors
w/ cheeses
breads
wines
croc./cheese fondues
etc.
Sandwiches